The Japane
An Int

The Japanese Language: An Introduction

A.E. Backhouse

Melbourne

OXFORD UNIVERSITY PRESS

Oxford Auckland New York

OXFORD UNIVERSITY PRESS

Oxford   New York   Toronto
Delhi   Bombay   Calcutta   Madras   Karachi
Kuala Lumpur   Singapore   Hong Kong   Tokyo
Nairobi   Dar es Salaam   Cape Town
Melbourne   Auckland   Madrid
and associated companies in
Berlin   Ibadan

National Library of Australia
Cataloguing-in-Publication data:

Backhouse, Anthony E. (Anthony Edgar), 1944–
  The Japanese language: an introduction.
  Bibliography.
  Index.
  ISBN 0 19 553509 X.
  1. Japanese language. 2. Japanese language—Textbooks for
  foreign speakers—English. I. Title.
495.682421

Edited by Cathryn Game
Indexed by Russell Brooks
Printed in Hong Kong by Elite
Published by Oxford University Press,
253 Normanby Road, South Melbourne, Australia

Contents

Tables

Figures

Preface

This book aims to provide an overview of the salient features of the Japanese language from the perspective of the English-speaking learner. It has been written primarily with undergraduate learners in mind; while the book is intended to be accessible to beginning students, some sections, particularly in later chapters, will be more meaningful on the basis of some grounding in the language. Beginners might therefore read the book initially for a general orientation and return later to these more detailed matters, and I hope that in this sense it may serve as a useful companion during continuing study. I hope that it will also be of interest to teachers of Japanese.

The book is a product of my own experience as a learner and teacher of Japanese and, naturally, its overall weighting and the selection of particular topics to some degree reflect my personal views and interests. Thus I have given more attention throughout to the spoken, rather than the written, language in the belief that a thorough grounding in the former provides the best general foundation for wider study. I have also devoted a good deal of space to discussion of vocabulary, the interest and importance of which are sometimes neglected.

The arrangement of the book is as follows. Chapter 1, Language and setting, is a preliminary chapter which deals briefly with the geographical, historical and social context of Japanese, and with its linguistic position vis-à-vis other languages of the world. Chapter 2, Sound, provides an account of the sound system of the language, with emphasis on contrasts with English in areas such as accentuation and rhythm as well as in vowels and consonants. A major feature of Japanese is its unique writing system, and chapter 3, Writing, deals with the main aspects of the structure and use of the component scripts, and also discusses the topic of romanization. The vocabulary of any foreign language tends to appear as a vast agglomeration of unrelated words, and the emphasis in chapter 4, Vocabulary, is on the various kinds of relationships and groupings found among Japanese lexical items.

Chapter 5, Grammar, presents an overview of Japanese grammar, focusing on the informal spoken language and dealing with the basic aspects of inflection, grammatical words and sentence structure. Finally, chapter 6, Discourse, attempts to fill in some of the gaps between the basic scheme described for the language and what happens when it is actually used on the ground; these include additional stylistic aspects of grammar, notably the formal style, and 'conversational' vocabulary items of various kinds. The reference section at the end of the book provides a list of materials recommended for reference and further reading.

Any book of this kind is heavily indebted to the work of others in the field; only some of this work is listed in the references, and I gratefully acknowledge this wider debt here. More specific thanks are due to Lesley Dow and her successor, Jill Lane, at Oxford University Press in Sydney for their help and advice throughout, to two anonymous readers for Oxford for their helpful comments on the manuscript, and to my wife, Kazuko, who typed much of the work and suggested several improvements to the text. Finally, like all teachers I have learned a great deal from the students to whom I have taught Japanese language and linguistics over the years, and who continue to embark in ever-growing numbers on the study of what remains a difficult and demanding language. If this book helps to elucidate their task, it will have achieved its purpose.

A.E. Backhouse

Note on transcription

The basic romanization system used for Japanese in this book is a variant of the Kunreishiki system (see table 3.3). Its additional features are that long vowels are written double (*oo*, etc.); long *e* is written everywhere as *ee* (rather than as *ei*); the syllable-final nasal is written *N*; *Ti* and *Di* represent the innovative sequences in words like *paaTii* 'party' and *Disuko* 'disco'; and the non-past form of the verb 'say' is written *yuu*. This system is employed throughout in citing Japanese linguistic forms and examples; these appear in italics, and capitals outside the basic symbols are used only at the beginning of sentences.

Elsewhere, Japanese terms used in the text (such as Kunreishiki, kanji, etc.) are given in Hepburn romanization, but again with long vowels written double. Ordinary Japanese names appearing as part of the English text also follow the Hepburn system, but without indication of long vowels (Tokyo, Sato, etc.).

Asterisks indicate ungrammatical forms or examples (*aranai*, *Anata wa uresii*, *difficultest*, etc.).

CHAPTER 1

LANGUAGE AND SETTING

This book is about the Japanese language. Much can be said about the structure and use of a language in isolation from considerations of the particular environment in which it has developed and in which it is used. Many features of languages everywhere are shared features, ultimately reflecting universal human cognitive mechanisms and social needs.

At the same time, individual languages evolve as systems of communication within particular communities, and in many details they carry the marks of their natural and social environment. This is often apparent in the vocabulary; in general, languages have words for concepts which its speakers find useful or important, and the 'lack of fit' between the meanings of many words in different languages indicates that these concepts vary. Languages also differ in the details of how they are used; much language behaviour is a form of social interaction, and we know that members of different societies do not always interact in the same way.

For such reasons, the serious study of a language can only benefit from a familiarity with its setting, and this is especially important in the case of languages which, like Japanese, lie outside our own cultural tradition. The aim of this preliminary chapter is to place Japanese in context by pointing, however briefly, to certain salient features of the Japanese physical and human environment which have helped shape, or which reflect, the world-view of its speakers. We also discuss the linguistic context of Japanese, looking at how it relates to other languages of the world, and consider the question of different types, or 'varieties', of Japanese.

Japan: The setting

It is important to begin this section by emphasizing the close nexus between the nation, Japan, and the language, Japanese. With very few exceptions, Japanese nationals speak Japanese; and conversely, with slightly more exceptions, speakers of Japanese are Japanese nationals. Such a nexus is far from universal across the languages of the world; in particular, it does not hold for English, which—in slightly different varieties—is the national language of several countries and has official status in many others, as well as being widely taught as the primary foreign language in many parts of the world (including Japan). By contrast, Japanese is very much the language of a single national entity, and this is reflected in various ways in Japanese language attitudes.

Geography

A glance at the map tells us that Japan is an island country lying at the eastern periphery of Asia. The four main islands extend in a north-east–south-west arc from Hokkaido in the north through Honshu, Shikoku and Kyushu. While Hokkaido, at its northernmost tip, lies within 50 km of the Russian island of Sakhalin, the coasts of western Honshu and northern

Kyushu are separated by almost 200 km of sea from the south-east corner of the Korean peninsula. The many smaller islands include the Ryukyu chain, which centres on Okinawa and stretches from southern Kyushu to within 150 km of Taiwan. In European terms, the main islands span the Mediterranean, extending from southern France to Morocco; on a North American scale, they stretch from Maine to Texas. The Japanese think of the country as extending north and west, from a central region around Tokyo. Northern Japan (*kitanihoN*) takes in Hokkaido and northern Honshu; eastern Japan (*higasinihoN*) central Honshu; and western Japan (*nisinihoN*) the western half of Honshu, Shikoku and Kyushu. A further important division is between the Japan Sea coast (*nihoNkaigawa*), facing the Asian continent, and the Pacific coast (*taiheeyoogawa*).

In area, Japan is slightly larger than Germany and somewhat smaller than California. Its population of 123 million, more than twice that of the United Kingdom, yields a notional population density of more than 300 people per square kilometre, already one of the highest in the world. Yet this figure does not take into account the highly mountainous nature of the country, which leads to the vast majority of this large population being packed into something like a sixth of its total area. As a result, Japan is the most crowded country of any size on earth, and this situation is further exacerbated by centralization in Tokyo and surrounding areas, which house some 30 million people. This accounts for the Japanese perception of Japan as a small (*semai*, literally 'constricted') country, and for the frequency of use of words centring on *komu* 'become crowded' and its opposite *suku* 'become uncrowded'. It is doubtless also responsible in no small measure for the Japanese concern for social discipline and restraint.

The Japanese climate is temperate, with hot, humid summers and relatively dry winters (although with heavy snowfalls on the Japan Sea coast), and the Japanese have traditionally been highly sensitive to the distinctions between the seasons and to their various natural and culinary associations. It is well known that Japan is highly prone to natural disasters. Apart from earthquake and volcanic activity, these also arise from the annual crop of typhoons that strike the country during summer and autumn, often causing landslides in the mountainous terrain.

In common with much of East and South-east Asia, Japan is a rice-producing nation, and rice, fish and other marine products, and vegetables—including the soya bean—have been the mainstays of the traditional diet. Naturally, these matters have clear linguistic repercussions and are reflected in the proliferation of basic terms in these areas. Thus rice is *ine* as a plant, *kome* as a commodity, *gohaN* or *mesi* as a boiled food; common types of edible seaweed include *koNbu* 'kelp', *nori* 'dried laver', *wakame* 'wakame'; and ubiquitous products of the soya bean include *syooyu* 'soy sauce', *toohu* 'bean curd' and *miso* '(fermented) bean paste'.

Modern Japan is a highly industrialized and urbanized society, and its major cities are concentrated along the seaboard of Honshu, facing the Pacific or, in western Japan, the Inland Sea. Starting from the north, these include Sendai in northern Honshu, Tokyo, Yokohama and Kawasaki in the Kanto region, Nagoya further west, Osaka and Kobe in Kansai and Hiroshima in western Honshu. Fukuoka and Kitakyushu are major cities on the northern coast of Kyushu. As exceptions to the general pattern, Sapporo in Hokkaido and the former capital of Kyoto in Kansai are major centres situated inland.

History

Summarized in a single sentence, the course of Japanese history has been marked by long centuries of isolation punctuated by rare but significant bursts of foreign influence. Japan's historical isolation, encouraged by its geographical position, has been reinforced by deliberate policies of seclusion.

The origins of the Japanese people are unclear, but it is generally agreed that the country was settled both by southern peoples, perhaps from southern China and farther afield, and by more northern continental strains. Japan is firmly located in the Chinese sphere of influence, and the first major wave of recorded cultural borrowing stems from this source. This influence became particularly marked during the sixth century, when Chinese civilization, including political and economic institutions as well as Buddhism, was enthusiastically embraced and led to the establishment, along Chinese lines, of the first capital cities in Nara (710) and Heiankyo (later Kyoto) (794). Importantly, the Japanese were introduced to writing by the Chinese, in the form of the character script which, as we shall see, was subsequently adapted by the Japanese to write their own language. More generally, Japanese familiarity with the Chinese language provided access to a rich source of lexical borrowing, and classical Chinese has continued to play this role—similar to that performed by Ancient Greek and Latin in Europe—down the centuries.

In the course of the Heian Period (794–1192), power shifted from the state into private hands, and the country gradually moved towards a feudal system from which it only emerged less than 150 years ago, with the opening of the country under pressure from the West. The most significant political development during this period was the unification of the country under the rule of the Tokugawa family from 1600 onwards. While Kyoto continued to be the nominal imperial capital, the Tokugawa shoguns ruled from Edo in eastern Japan. The Edo (or Tokugawa) Period was marked by internal stability and by a policy of national seclusion. Western missionaries and traders had first reached Japan in the 1540s, but the influence of Christianity in particular alarmed Japan's rulers, and under the Tokugawas the Western presence was restricted to a Dutch trading post in Nagasaki in Kyushu. Undisturbed by external pressures, this was an age of national consolidation notable for economic growth and generally efficient government informed by a Confucianist ideology. Inevitably, however, the country fell behind the West in technological, including military, development, and when confronted by United States ships in 1853, Japan was forced to open the country to foreign trade.

The next stage of Japan's history was dominated by the drive to modernize the country and to achieve equality with the Western powers. The end of the Tokugawa Shogunate formally came in 1868, and under the Meiji Restoration the imperial capital was moved to Edo, renamed Tokyo. In the ensuing period of rapid social, political and economic change, the old class divisions were abolished, new government institutions were established on European models and new industries were developed. Overseas, Japan's defeat of China in the Sino-Japanese War resulted in its annexation of Taiwan in 1895; its victory over the Russians in 1905 further extended its influence, and Korea was annexed in 1910. Having formed an alliance with Britain in 1902, Japan took its place among the victors of World War I as a powerful modern state.

Subsequent political instability and economic insecurity led to the ascendancy of the military and to expansionist policies abroad, firstly in Manchuria, then in China and finally in South-east Asia and the Pacific. Japan was defeated in 1945, and the subsequent American occupation represented its first experience of foreign hegemony. In general, this partnership was successfully negotiated, as was the accompanying spate of change faced by the country for the second time in less than a century. Post-war Japan has been dominated by the pursuit and achievement of economic prosperity. It is currently negotiating the challenge of a successful transition to broader participation in the international community, on whose stability its future well-being so crucially depends.

Society

A brief introduction can do no more than mention some of the more salient features of mainstream Japanese society; while these must be acknowledged as broad stereotypes, their wide recognition suggests that they have some validity at this level. The area is certainly of the highest significance for language students. In Japan, we find a strong cultural preoccupation with social relationships, and this is clearly reflected in the language, where distinctions of social distance—both horizontal (in terms of the degree of familiarity between the speaker and the addressee) and vertical (in terms of deference paid by the speaker to the person talked about)—are systematically marked in grammar and vocabulary, and where many greetings and other social formulas make explicit reference to social ties and obligations.

Virtually all descriptions of Japanese society refer to the group orientation of the Japanese. Human beings everywhere exist in social groups, but the fact of social interdependence is accorded clear acknowledgement in Japanese culture. Among the groups of which the Japanese are typically members, the most obvious are the family or close kin group (*kazoku/miuti*), close friends—centrally drawn from among classmates from school or university days—(*tomodati*), and the workplace group (*dooryoo*). Close kin and close friends may collectively be referred to as 'familiars': these provide the individual's most intimate relationships, and are linguistically set apart in that members interact in informal style. Further afield, the individual has social relations with various other persons, often through cross-group contact. Beyond these are 'outsiders' (*taniN*), who may be thought of as constituting the mass of society outside the individual's social sphere.

The group membership of participants has important consequences for language interaction. Broadly speaking, language use within groups is determined by hierarchical relations, with juniors deferring to seniors; thus, even within an intimate group such as the family, terms of address and reference for family members reflect seniority with, for example, younger siblings employing deferential kin terms for the eldest brother and eldest sister (*oniisaN*, *oneesaN*, etc.) rather than given names. In communication across groups, the tendency is for each group to defer to the other. The labels 'in-group' and 'out-group' are often applied to Japanese communication in this context; these are to be understood as relative terms, referring to the direction of communication with respect to particular subject matters. Thus, where one is talking about one's family members, in-group communication refers to communication within one's own family. Communication directed outside the family on this topic is by definition out-group, and in this case deferential terms such as *oniisaN* and *oneesaN* for one's own kin are replaced by non-deferential terms such as *ani*, *ane*, etc.

More generally, life for many Japanese certainly involves the commitment of a large amount of time and energy to social interaction within groups, particularly workplace groups. Group membership provides the primary reference of personal identification in many settings. It also gives access, through the personal connections of other group members, to a wider range of social networks, a highly significant function in a country which, in a very real sense, runs on personal contacts. Group solidarity is reinforced by frequent interaction in a variety of activities, and group-scale socializing is a familiar component of the Japanese scene. This focus on group interaction imparts a somewhat clannish quality to Japanese society. While social relations and expectations are clearly codified within the structure of the group, casual interaction with outsiders (*taniN*) receives correspondingly low attention.

The majority of groups are hierarchically structured, with rank primarily determined by seniority, and here again the clear Japanese acknowledgement of hierarchy as part of the social order is often contrasted with the more egalitarian ethic of many Western societies. As we have indicated, ranking influences interpersonal behaviour, including language behaviour, within the group. However, hierarchy does not imply authoritarianism; seniors are expected to show consideration for the welfare of their juniors, and group decisions, for example, are generally canvassed among all members rather than being imposed from the top. Moreover, since ranking is essentially based on age, it may not necessarily reflect capability and merit, and this may be recognized privately. It is, however, an important principle that form must be maintained publicly, particularly in external dealings of the group. This is one aspect of the oft-cited pragmatic Japanese ability to separate 'formal' or 'official' reality (*tatemae*) from private knowledge or opinions (*hoNne*) and indeed of the general importance attached to maintaining the appearance of following established forms. It is also important to understand that personal hierarchies are defined within the framework of a given group or situation, and not for society as a whole in terms of, say, social class. The same person will be a senior in one setting but a junior in another and will adjust his or her behaviour accordingly, but these are situational matters. In terms of society as a whole—with the notable exception of some minority groups—consciousness of general class differences is less pronounced than in many European societies.

Overall, Japanese society encourages the development of disciplined individuals who know their place and observe the conventions, and it rewards conformist values. The Japanese virtues are the old-fashioned virtues of group loyalty, role commitment and diligence, and there is little admiration for individual flamboyance or for deviation from established patterns. It is recognized that submission to societal forms and channels involves some repression of individuality, and the exercise of *gamaN* ('stoicism, endurance') in this respect is universally perceived as a strength, not a weakness. Much of Japanese life follows an established, shared script, and its persistence clearly underlies the country's continuing strengths in the areas of social discipline and group action. Conformity also underlies the Japanese propensity for nationwide booms and fads, be they in fashion, sports, travel or whatever; in a society that values shared experience and predictability, following the crowd in such matters is no bad thing.

Finally we must mention the Japanese consciousness of ethnic and cultural—including linguistic—uniqueness. Clearly, all human societies show similarities as well as differences, but it is significant that the Japanese have often sought to emphasize the features which set them apart from other peoples and cultures. Various reasons may be discerned for this. Historically Japan's forced emergence from 250 years of national seclusion is still relatively recent, and even today Japan's population of more than 120 million includes less than a million foreign residents, three-quarters of whom are ethnic Koreans and Chinese. It may also be interpreted as a defence mechanism against Western cultural influence; in practice, 'unique' often means different from the West or—in matters of language—different from English, although it is extremely important to note that Japan's cultural traditions have largely persisted despite superficial Westernization. Finally, it may be seen as a reflection of the 'us–them' syndrome implicit in Japan's group-oriented social structure, from which perspective non-Japanese are the ultimate outsiders. Most importantly, all this does not preclude individual foreigners from being accepted as members of groups, but it does mean that they must be prepared to encounter various stereotypes at the level of Japanese society as a whole.

Japanese: The language

Japanese is the native language of more than 120 million speakers, and in these terms it ranks in the top half-dozen languages in the world. The growth of Japan's economic influence has also brought expansion in the study of Japanese as a foreign language, most notably in China and South Korea, but also in South-east Asia, Australasia and North America. However, this is still a relatively recent development and, as we have seen, Japanese remains very much the language of Japan. Where does this language come from, and how does it relate to the languages of the world? Furthermore, labels such as 'Japanese' in fact cover a range of different types, or 'varieties', of a language. What varieties of Japanese are there?

Wider relations

Different languages may or may not be genetically related, in the sense of having developed historically from a common 'parent' language. Similarities between languages may derive from genetic kinship, but they may also arise in other ways; they may be due to chance (languages, after all, fall into a limited number of types), or they may be due to cultural influence of one language on the other.

The only genetic relationship that has been established beyond doubt for Japanese is with the languages of the Ryukyu Islands to the south; these languages are mutually unintelligible with Japanese, and indeed in some cases among themselves. However, they are more commonly considered as dialects of Japanese, rather than as separate languages; the language/dialect distinction is often based on political rather than linguistic considerations and, although Ryukyu was historically an independent kingdom, it has long been politically absorbed into Japan. Beyond this case, the origins of Japanese—as of the Japanese people—remain obscure. Various genetic links have been proposed, most plausibly with Korean, but proof of genetic relationship depends on the establishment of systematic sound correspondences between the languages concerned, and it is not generally agreed that these have been clearly demonstrated. Interestingly, this unclear genetic status is shared by the closest geographical neighbours of Japanese, namely Korean and Ainu (formerly spoken in Hokkaido and Sakhalin, but now virtually extinct).

The question of genetic relationship must not be equated with the general question of similarity between languages. While it might seem that genetically related languages should be superficially similar, this is not necessarily the case, since separation from the parent language may date back thousands of years, during which time the two descendants may diverge dramatically. Conversely, similarities between languages may be due to other reasons. In the first place, they may be purely typological, i.e. due to the fact that, in one or more respects, the two languages happen to exemplify the same structural 'type' of language. At the level of sound systems, for example, many languages from different parts of the world are 'tone languages', making systematic use of differences of pitch to distinguish between different words. Languages have commonly been classified with regard to morphology, or word structure: in this respect Japanese is usually described as an agglutinating language, favouring a structure in which clearly identifiable meaningful 'bits' (or 'morphemes') are strung together to form often quite long words, as illustrated in commonplace examples such as *tabe-sase-rare-ta* ('eat' + causative + passive + past tense) 'was made to eat'. Languages also fall into various syntactic types, based on the ways in which they combine words into sentences. In terms of word order, for example, English says *The mouse ate the cheese*, whereas Japanese has *Nezumi ga tiizu o tabeta* ('Mouse cheese ate'): based on sentences of this kind, English is said to be an SVO (subject + verb + object) language, whereas Japanese is SOV. As it happens, SOV appears to be the most common pattern across the languages of the world; whereas English has prepositions, SOV languages normally have 'postpositions' (like *ga* and *o* in the examples above), and Japanese is a highly typical language of this type. So too is Korean, and the two languages share striking similarities in syntax—although there are also some significant differences.

Finally, similarities between languages may arise from direct cultural contact, in the form of borrowing, irrespective of genetic or typological relationships. At least in earlier stages of history, this type of influence obviously arises between languages in relatively close geographical proximity, and we have already referred to Chinese as a major source of borrowing dating back some 1500 years. Korean has also been heavily influenced by Chinese—like Japanese, both in its vocabulary and its writing system—so that this provides a further point of contact between these two languages. The second major cultural influence on Japanese has come from Western languages, in recent times overwhelmingly from English. Indeed, Japanese has been a heavy borrower and, as we shall see in chapter 4, this has resulted in a clear compartmentalization of its vocabulary. As a source of borrowing itself, Japanese has been less influential. The main exceptions include, interestingly, Chinese—where many Sino-Japanese terms coined in Japan during the Meiji Period were subsequently 'reborrowed' into Chinese—and languages of Micronesia such as Ponapean, Saipanese and Yapese; these territories were formerly German possessions and came under Japanese mandate following World War I.

Varieties

As with all languages, it is possible and useful to distinguish between various 'types' of Japanese. In the first place, Japanese varies geographically, and we have seen that the dialects of the Ryukyu Islands, for example, are mutually unintelligible with 'mainland' Japanese. Some other dialects, such as those of northern Honshu, are also difficult to understand for outsiders. As in many other countries, however, local Japanese dialects are losing their vigour under the influence of education and mass communication, and in many settings they give way to more orthodox varieties which may still preserve some regional features but which level out extreme dialect differences. The language of the Tokyo area is the most influential of these regional spoken languages, and it is characterized by its own particular features of pronunciation, grammar and vocabulary.

However, 'Tokyo Japanese', as we may call it, is not to be equated with Standard Japanese. As part of the process of modernization, most nations select, or construct, one variety to serve as *the* official representative variety at the national level, to be used, for example, in school textbooks, newspapers and national broadcasting. In the case of Japan, historically this variety was based predominantly on the language of Tokyo, though with an admixture of features of Kansai Japanese, where the language of the traditional capital, Kyoto, in particular, carried prestige. Some of these features are also present in Tokyo regional speech, but it is important to realize that standard languages are primarily written languages and that, as such, they naturally show some differences from spoken languages; writing and speech fulfil different functions, and this is reflected in the structure of the mediums through which they are effected. Thus all languages have colloquial (i.e. spoken-language) and bookish (written-language) vocabulary, and commonly there are also accompanying grammatical differences. In short, spoken and written languages are to be regarded as distinct, although overlapping, varieties; in the present case, Tokyo Japanese belongs within the former and Standard Japanese within the latter.

In the following chapters we look more closely at individual aspects of 'Japanese'. While much of our description will relate to the common overlapping core, we shall distinguish where necessary between 'spoken (i.e. Tokyo) Japanese' and 'written (i.e. Standard) Japanese'. We begin with the sound system, which is that of Tokyo Japanese, but which also constitutes 'received' pronunciation of Standard Japanese in its spoken uses, as in news broadcasting.

CHAPTER

2 SOUND

Every language has its own characteristic sound system. Most obviously, each language makes use of a particular set of individual sounds and combines these in particular ways into larger sound groupings such as syllables. Languages also differ in terms of the features of the sound 'envelope' in which these combinations are wrapped: matters such as word stress or accentuation, and the rhythm and intonation of connected speech.

Achieving a good pronunciation of a foreign language requires mastery of each of these aspects and involves the acquisition of a complex set of new habits. In this we are clearly influenced by the sound patterns of our native language, as illustrated by the demonstrable presence of typical 'accents' in the English of foreign speakers. While Japanese presents us with fewer difficulties in pronunciation than many other languages, several areas need careful attention; as we shall see, in addition to particular individual sounds, these include the general distinction between short and long vowels and consonants, and the need to avoid English-style stress.

There can be no question of mastering the pronunciation of any language purely from a textbook. This can only be achieved on the basis of exposure to natural speech and of uninhibited imitation of native speakers. However, our efforts will be better directed if based on an awareness and understanding of the problems involved, and the aim of this chapter is to present the main features of standard Tokyo-based Japanese pronunciation, paying particular attention to problem areas for English-speaking learners.

Sounds and syllables

Individual Japanese sounds are conveniently discussed within the framework of the syllable. Japanese syllables are either short or long, and each type has a relatively simple structure.

Short syllables

We begin with short syllables. A Japanese short syllable may consist of a vowel alone, a single consonant plus a vowel, or a consonant plus a vowel with an intervening semivowel (y):

$$\text{Short syllable} = \begin{cases} \text{Vowel (V)} \\ or \\ \text{Consonant + vowel (CV)} \\ or \\ \text{Consonant + semivowel + vowel (C}y\text{ V)} \end{cases}$$

Below we take up these individual sounds in turn.

Vowels

$$V: \quad \boxed{a \quad i \quad u \quad e \quad o}$$

Japanese has five short vowels, as shown. (By this we mean five short vowel *sounds*; our concern throughout this chapter is with sounds. English is sometimes said to have 'five vowels', but this refers to vowel *letters* of the alphabet, and in fact English has many more vowel sounds: the letter *u*, for example, represents different vowel sounds in the words *but* and *put*.)

These Japanese vowels are pure, which is to say that they do not involve a change in sound quality during their pronunciation; in this they contrast with many English vowels, such as the vowels in *see*, *sue*, *say* and *so*, which in most accents of English are diphthongs and do involve such a change. Also (with one exception noted below), Japanese vowels are given their full pronunciation wherever they occur; each *a* in the word *sakana* is pronounced alike, and there is no 'weak' vowel in Japanese comparable to the English sound at the beginning of *about*.

The individual vowels are discussed and illustrated below. Since it is generally impossible to describe sounds with full precision in writing, we include reference to International Phonetic Association (IPA) phonetic symbols (enclosed in square brackets) where appropriate.

a: Similar to the Northern English vowel in *cap*, intermediate between IPA [a] and [ɑ].

ka   aka   saka   sakana   gasagasa

i: Similar to the French vowel in *si*, symbol [i].

mi   imi   mimi   migi-ni   nikibi

u: This vowel is unrounded [ɯ] and requires careful attention. To produce it, pronounce English *u* as in *cushion* but without rounding or protruding of the lips, like a ventriloquist. We shall see that weak lip activity of this kind is a common general feature of Japanese pronunciation.

umu   sugu   sumu   nusumu   bukubuku

e: Between [e] and [ɛ]. Not a diphthong as in English *say*.

te   te-de   nete   semete   hebereke

o: Between [o] and [ɔ]. Not over-rounded, and not a diphthong as in English *so*.

mo   oto   koto   kodomo   kosokoso

In a succession of vowels, each vowel essentially preserves its individual pronunciation:

ai   au   aoi   ie   ue   ei   oi   ou

There is one important variation in the pronunciation of short vowels, namely devoicing, which chiefly affects *i* and *u*. Basically, these vowels are pronounced without voice, or whispered, when they occur between two voiceless consonants (*k, s, t, h, p*), or after a voiceless consonant and before a pause (as at the end of a sentence). In the following words, the vowel marked with a slash is normally devoiced (IPA symbols [i̥] and [ɯ̥], respectively):

ki̸ku   ki̸ta   ku̸sa   su̸ki   su̸pai

In some cases of devoicing, the vowel may seem to be completely lacking; *suki*, for example, may sound like [ski]. The general strategy should nevertheless be to pronounce the vowel, though whispered, and we will see that the full effect of the basic vowel is often reflected in the pronunciation of the preceding consonant. Note that the final *u* in the common forms *desu* and *-masu* will be devoiced when these end sentences.

While speakers from some parts of Japan pronounce *suki*, etc. with fully voiced vowels, devoicing is a prominent feature of standard pronunciation.

Consonants

Table 2.1 Consonant + vowel short syllables

CV:											
k/g	ka	ki	ku	ke	ko	ga	gi		gu	ge	go
s/z	sa	si(shi)	su	se	so	za	zi(ji)		zu	ze	zo
t/d	ta	ti(chi)	tu(tsu)	te	to	da				de	do
n	na	ni	nu	ne	no						
h/b/p	ha	hi	hu(fu)	he	ho	ba	bi		bu	be	bo
						pa	pi		pu	pe	po
m	ma	mi	mu	me	mo						
y	ya		yu		yo						
r	ra	ri	ru	re	ro						
w	wa										

Japanese short syllables with the shape consonant plus vowel (CV) are set out in table 2.1 above, in the conventional arrangement of the kana syllabaries (comparable to English alphabetical order). Each syllable consists of one of the five vowels preceded by one of the consonants listed at the left of the table.

General features of the pronunciation of Japanese consonants include, once again, the avoidance of lip protrusion in certain sounds. Excessive aspiration should also be avoided. Aspiration is manifested in the puff of breath that follows the initial consonants in English words like *pin*, *tin*, *kin*, etc.; by contrast, Japanese *p*, *t* and *k* are only very lightly aspirated. Finally, many Japanese consonants are noticeably palatalized, i.e. pronounced as if followed by a short intervening *y* sound, before the vowel *i*.

k: Very light aspiration. Palatalized ([k^j]) before *i*.

ke   kono   nuku   kusuri   kimono

g: Basically similar to English, but palatalized ([g^j]) before *i*. Some speakers pronounce *g* as [ŋ]—i.e. as *ng* in standard

English *sing*—within words (as opposed to word-initially); though not uncommon, this pronunciation appears to be losing ground among younger speakers and, while they should be prepared to hear it, learners may ignore this variant in their own speech.

ga   gogo   geta   kagi   oyogu

s: Similar to English except before *i*.

sa   soko   mise   sumu   sᵤsumu

Before *i* it resembles the *sh* sound in English *shin* but is pronounced with the blade of the tongue raised closer to the palate than for the English sound and without accompanying lip protrusion (IPA symbol [ɕ]). Learners may begin by aiming to produce a palatalized *s* sound in this combination, i.e. [sʲi]. (The syllable *si* is represented as *shi* in some systems of romanization.)

sima   siba   sᵢka   sasimi   kimasᵢta

z: Similar to English except before *i*, but pronounced [dz] as in English *lids* after *N* and commonly at the beginning of words.

zu   kaze   mizu   biza   aNzu

Before *i* it resembles the affricate consonant in English *judge* ([dʒ]) but, as with *s*, the blade of the tongue is raised closer to the palate and there is no accompanying lip protrusion. (*zi* is sometimes romanized as *ji*.)

zi   ziko   azi   yozi   kaNzi

t: Before *a*, *e* and *o*, very light aspiration. Tongue contact is further forward than for English *t*, with the tongue tip against the back of the upper front teeth and the blade against the gums.

te   take   tobu   tabete   tomato

Before *i* it resembles the affricate consonant in English *church* ([tʃ]), but is produced in similar fashion to Japanese *z* before *i*, of which it is the voiceless counterpart. No lip protrusion. (*ti* is sometimes romanized as *chi*.)

tizu   tigau   t̸kai   itido   itiniti

Before *u*, *t* is pronounced [ts] as in English *cats*. English-speakers need to practise making this sound at the beginning of words. (*tu* is sometimes romanized as *tsu*.)

itu   tugi   t̸ki   t̸ti   t̸kuru

d: Occurs only before *a*, *e* and *o*. Tongue contact with upper teeth and gums, as for Japanese *t*.

dete   dame   doko   koko-de   dabudabu

n: Tongue contact as for Japanese *t* and *d*. Palatalized ([nʲ]) before *i*.

naka   neko   kono   koko-ni   nikoniko

h: Similar to English before *a*, *e*, *o*.

ha   hada   heta   hone   hosoboso

Before *i*, *h* is pronounced like the German *ch* sound in *ich* (IPA symbol [ç]). This sound has considerable friction and is often heard as the initial sound of English words like *huge*.

hiza   hima   h̸to   h̸kari   higasi

Before *u*, *h* is pronounced as a bilabial voiceless fricative ([ɸ]). This sound does not exist in English; unlike English *f*, which involves friction between the upper teeth and the lower lip, the Japanese sound is made by blowing air between the two lips, as if blowing out a candle. (*hu* is sometimes romanized as *fu*.)

hue   humu   hune   h̸ta   h̸kumu

b: Similar to English. Palatalized ([bʲ]) before *i*.

obi   haba   kabe   bikini   bosoboso

p: Very light aspiration. Palatalized ([pʲ]) before *i*.

papa   piano   pokapoka   p̸kap̸ka   potapota

m: Similar to English. Palatalized ([mʲ]) before *i*.

me   umi   yomu   mado   kumo

y: As in English *yet* (symbol [j]). Occurs only before *a, u, o*.

yamu   huyu   yomu   moya   yoboyobo

r: This is perhaps the most difficult individual Japanese sound for English-speakers to acquire. The Japanese *r* is technically a tap (IPA symbol [ɾ]), produced by the tongue tip flicking the alveolar ridge (the hard gum ridge slightly behind the upper teeth) in a forward and downward movement. It is quite different from English *r* sounds (commonly [ɹ]), and these must be avoided at all costs, an English *l* sound being generally preferable. The best strategy is for learners to aim at producing a *light*, *rapid* English *d*, and the sound required is often heard in the casual pronunciation of words like *better* associated with American English. At the beginning of words (after pause), the tongue tip in the Japanese sound is already touching the alveolar ridge before being released, and the resemblance to an English *d* here is very close.

kara   huro   razio   retasu   hirihiri

w: Only occurs before *a*. Similar to English but, predictably, pronounced without lip protrusion. IPA symbol [ɰ].

wara   niwa   wakaru   watasi-wa   warawareru

Consonants plus *y*

Table 2.2 Consonant + *y* + vowel short syllables

CyV:						
ky/gy	*kya*	*kyu*	*kyo*	*gya*	*gyu*	*gyo*
sy/zy	*sya(sha)*	*syu(shu)*	*syo(sho)*	*zya(ja)*	*zyu(ju)*	*zyo(jo)*
ty	*tya(cha)*	*tyu(chu)*	*tyo(cho)*			
ny	*nya*	*nyu*	*nyo*			
hy/by/py	*hya*	*hyu*	*hyo*	*bya*	*byu*	*byo*
				pya	*pyu*	*pyo*
my	*mya*	*myu*	*myo*			
ry	*rya*	*ryu*	*ryo*			

Short syllables of the shape consonant plus *y* plus vowel (C*y*V) are shown in table 2.2. These syllables involve all consonants except *d* and *w* and the vowels *a*, *u* and *o*. The most important general point concerning their pronunciation is that they are *single, short* syllables: *kya* is not pronounced as [kia] (i.e. as two syllables), but as [kja], rhyming with *ka* and of similar length. In general the intervening *y* has a similar effect on the pronunciation of preceding consonants as *i*; these are palatalized or, in the case of *s*, *z*, *t* and *h*, subject to the more dramatic modifications already described. Major points of pronunciation are summarized below.

ky: *k* palatalized, *y* voiceless, with some friction ([kj̥]).

    kyaku   kyabetu   kyoka   kyoku   kyorokyoro

sy: Pronounced as Japanese *s* when before *i* ([ɕ]), i.e. roughly like English *sh* but with more tongue height and without lip protrusion. (*sy* is sometimes romanized as *sh*.)

    kaisya   syumi   gesyuku   syokuzi   syabusyabu

zy: As Japanese *z* when before *i*. (*zy* is sometimes romanized as *j*.)

    zyaguti   pazyama   zyuku   kanozyo   zyarazyara

ty: As Japanese *t* when before *i*. (*ty* is sometimes romanized as *ch*.)

    otya   tyanoma   tyosya   metyakutya   tyorotyoro

hy: As *h* in English *huge*, with some friction ([çj̥]).

    hyaku   nihyaku   gohyaku   nanahyaku   hyorohyoro

py: *p* palatalized, *y* voiceless, with some friction ([pj̥]).

    pyokopyoko

ry: *r* as rapid English *d*.

    sakuryaku   miryoku   ryakusu   ryokutya   ryohi

Long syllables

Long syllables in Japanese have the following basic structure:

$$\text{Long syllable} = \text{Short syllable} + \begin{cases} \text{Final vowel (v)} \\ or \\ \text{Final nasal } (N) \\ or \\ \text{Final consonant (c)} \end{cases}$$

That is to say, a Japanese short syllable (of the shape V, CV or C*y*V) can be lengthened in one of three ways: by a further vowel, by the nasal sound *N*, or by a syllable-final consonant. Below we look at each of these in turn.

Long vowels

For pronunciation purposes, the most important type of vowel-extended syllables involve long vowels. All Japanese vowel sounds occur long (i.e. doubled) as well as short, and this is a vital distinction in the sound system of the language. In long vowels (*aa, ii, uu, ee, oo*) the sound is simply prolonged for twice the length of the corresponding short vowel with, most importantly, no variation in quality; i.e. Japanese long vowels are pure. Unlike short vowels, long vowels are never devoiced. (Long vowels are sometimes romanized with macrons, as $\bar{a}, \bar{i}, \bar{u}, \bar{e}, \bar{o}$.)

aa: *aa baa saa manaa maamaa*

ii: *ii sŭkii biiru tiisai takŭsii*

uu: Unrounded, as a ventriloquist ([ɯː]).

   yuu ruu kuuki huuhu aayuu

ee: *ee eega gakŭsee teenee meekaa*

oo: *koo soo kyoo ryokoo koohii*

Syllable-final nasal

Short syllables may also be extended by the addition of *N*. This is an unreleased nasal sound, whose precise pronunciation varies from consonant-like to vowel-like according to the sounds which surround it. It is important to realize that this sound is quite long; the syllable *kaN*, for example, is roughly twice as long as the short syllable *ka*. (*N* is commonly romanized as *n* and, in certain positions, sometimes as *m*.)

Before *b*, *p*, *m*, it is pronounced [m]. *Nm* is thus pronounced as a long *m*.

koNbu saNpo eNpĮtu hoN-mo saNmai

Before *z*, *t*, *d*, *n*, *r*, it is pronounced [n]. *Nn* is thus pronounced as a long *n*. Tongue against the teeth and gums for *Nt*, *Nd*, *Nn*.

aNzu kaNzi ziNzya daNti koNdo doNna beNri

Before *k*, *g*, it is pronounced [ŋ]. *Nk* and *Ng* are thus pronounced as *nk* and *ng* in the English words *banker* and *finger*.

geNki meNkyo beNkyoo nihoNgo oNgaku

Before pause (as at the end of a sentence), it is pronounced as an unreleased velar nasal. To produce this sound, learners should aim to pronounce (a rather long) *ng* as in English *sing* ([ŋ]), but stop short of the final part of this sound: in the Japanese sound there is no contact between the back of the tongue and the roof of the mouth.

sumimaseN arimaseN wakarimaseN

Elsewhere (i.e. before *s*, *h*, *y*, *w* and vowels), *N* is pronounced as a nasalized vowel, often as nasalized *i* ([ĩ]) or *u* ([ũ]) depending on the surrounding sounds. These are difficult sounds for English-speakers and require careful attention. A common serious fault is to pronounce *N* here as *n*, but in none of the Japanese variants is contact made between the tongue and the roof of the mouth. Once again, a good beginning strategy is to aim at a contact-free [ŋ]-sound as above, and close attention should be paid to the pronunciation of native speakers.

riNsu   deNsya   maNneNhįtu   iNhure   hoNya   hoN-wa
nihoN-e   hoN-o   maNiN   seNeN

Syllable-final consonant

Lastly, a short syllable may be lengthened by the addition of a final consonant. Like *N*, this may be regarded as a single sound that varies according to the sound which follows it (and, like *N*, it is written with a single symbol in the kana syllabaries). This sound is actually the first part of a geminate (i.e. doubled) consonant. In Japanese, *k*, *s*, *t* and *p* commonly occur in this form (*kk*, *ss*, *tt*, *pp*); to pronounce them, simply prolong the closure (for *kk*, *tt*, *pp*) or the sibilant (hissing) sound (for *ss*) for the length of an ordinary short syllable. Once again, this is an important distinction, and a common error is to make these sounds insufficiently long. Note that *kk*, *tt* and *pp* are unaspirated, i.e. pronounced without any following puff of breath.

kk: Slightly longer than the long *k*-sound in English *back-cut*. Palatalized before *i* and *y*.

makka   sakki   kekkyoku   makkuro   kekkoN

ss: Compare the long *s* sound in English *misspell*. Long [ɕ] before *i* and in combination with *y*.

assari   zassi   hassya   massugu   kossori

tt: Slightly longer than the long *t* sound in English *flat-top*, and with the tongue against the teeth and gums. Before *i* and in combination with *y*, it resembles the *t-ch* sequence ([ttʃ]) in English *hot chili*, and before *u* it is pronounced [tts]. (*tti* is sometimes romanized as *tchi*.)

batta   matti   mattya   yottu   sotto

pp: Compare the long *p* sound in English *chip-pan*. Palatalized before *i* and *y*.

rippa   ippįki   happyaku   kįppu   sįppo

This concludes our survey of long syllables in Japanese. We have seen that each type of short syllable (V, CV, CyV) can be lengthened in three ways:

	V(i)	CV(ko)	CyV(zyu)
Add v	ii	koo	$zyuu$
Add N	iN	koN	$zyuN$
Add c	$ip(po)$	$kot(ti)$	$zyuk(ko)$

Short syllables, and each of the lengthening elements (v, N, c), are said to constitute one 'mora' in Japanese. The mora is actually the unit of metre in traditional Japanese poetry (where lines must consist of e.g. five or seven moras), and there is a broad correlation between the number of moras and the time-length of a word. Long syllables thus consist of two moras, and it is important for our pronunciation that we aim at ensuring that they occupy twice the time of short syllables.

Contrasting sounds and syllables

To conclude this section we give some examples of important sound contrasts that call for listening and production practice.

ki/ku, vowels devoiced: *k̩si/k̩si k̩sya/k̩syami k̩tta/k̩tta*

si/syu: *siryuu/syuryuu nihoNsi/nihoNsyu s̩kkoo/sy̩kkoo k̩si/k̩syu*

zi/zyu: *zigyoo/zyugyoo   zippuN/zyuppuN   zisiN/zyusiN zeNzitsu/zeNzyutu*

su/tu: *suna/tuna suzuri/tuzuri s̩ku/t̩ku s̩ki/t̩ki hanasu/hanatu surusuru/turuturu*

si/hi, sy/hy: *simo/himo siiru/hiiru s̩ku/h̩ku s̩kaku/h̩kaku syoomeN/hyoomeN syoozyoo/hyoozyoo syoohi/hyoosi*

d/r: *hidoi/hiroi kudoi/kuroi sode/sore koNdo/koNro naNraka/ naN-da-ka doku/roku daNboo/raNboo deNpoo/reNpoo rakudai/ rakurai midareru/mirareru daradara n/N*: *tani/taNi sono/soN-o kineN/kiNeN kanyuu/kaNyuu*

a/aa: *kado/kaado obasaN/obaasaN*

i/ii: *biru/biiru ozisaN/oziisaN*

u/uu: *kuki/kuuki syuto/syuuto*

e/ee: *suteki/suteeki sekeN/seekeN*

o/oo: *toru/tooru onosaN/oonosaN*

k/kk: *saki/sakki makura/makkura*

s/ss: *masu/massugu bisyobisyo/bissyori*

t/tt: *mati/matti kite/kitte*

p/pp: *supai/suppai papa-to/pappa-to*

short/long syllables, various: *koko/kookoo mata/maNtaN ito/ittoo yume/yuumee yokka/yooka ryokoo/ryooko suupu/suupuuN mekka/meekaa syottyuu/syootyuu kita/kitta/kiita saka/sakka/sakkaa isyoo/issyo/issyoo*

Word accentuation

The total sound shape of a Japanese word involves more than its vowels and consonants. Despite their identical make-up, the words *kaki* 'oyster' and *kaki* 'persimmon' are pronounced differently. In 'oyster' the first syllable has a higher pitch than the second, while in 'persimmon' the second syllable is higher. Japanese words carry an accentual contour.

English words have somewhat similar properties. The word *extract* accented on the first syllable is a noun (as in *an extract from a book*) and on the second syllable a verb (*extract a tooth*). It is sometimes said that Japanese accentuation is mainly a matter of pitch (i.e. high/low), and English accentuation more a matter of loudness or stress (i.e. heavy/light). While this is an oversimplification of the facts, it has some value as a broad characterization. Impressionistically, accentuation in Japanese is much lighter than in English, where stressed and unstressed vowels often differ substantially in quality (cf. the vowels in *photograph* vs *photography*). This is a major difference between the sound systems of the two languages, and learners need to make a conscious effort to avoid imposing English-style stress patterns on to Japanese.

The standard Tokyo-based accentual system makes use of two levels of relative pitch. In the representations below, ⌐ marks a change from higher to lower pitch; ⌐ from lower to higher:

> *ka⌐ki* 'oyster'
> *ka⌐ki* 'persimmon'
> *ta⌐bako* 'cigarette'
> *ta⌐ma⌐go* 'egg'
> *a⌐rima⌐su* 'there is/are'
> *a⌐rimase⌐N* 'there is/are not'

The two other basic principles of the system are that the first two moras in a word are always at different pitch levels, and that there can be no more than a single drop of pitch within a word. Auditorily, the clearest effect of accentual contours occurs where there is a drop in pitch from higher to lower: the last mora before the drop (*ka* in *ka⌐ki*, *ma* in *ta⌐ma⌐go* and *a⌐rima⌐su*, *se* in *a⌐rimase⌐N*) is heard as (lightly) accented; words such as *ka⌐ki* and *ta⌐bako* have no drop in pitch, and thus no mora is heard as accented in this way. Words may be accented on the final mora, as *si⌐ma⌐* 'island'. In isolation, such words have an identical contour to unaccented words (such as *ka⌐ki*), but the difference becomes clear in connected speech when they are followed by particles: in the phrase *si⌐ma⌐-o*, *ma* is followed by a drop in pitch and is heard as accented, whereas in *ka⌐ki-o* the pitch remains high.

A notable effect of word accentuation is that the contour of a composite word often differs substantially from that of its individual components. For example, when names of cities are combined with the suffix *-si* 'city', the resulting words are accented on the next to last syllable, irrespective of their original contour:

Yo⌐kohama⌐/Yo⌐kohama⌐si
Kyo⌐oto/Kyo⌐oto⌐si
Wa⌐ka⌐yama/Wa⌐kayama⌐si

Compound words may also be affected in this way:

mi⌐nato 'harbour' + ma⌐ti⌐ 'town'/ mi⌐natoma⌐ti 'port town'
ni⌐hoNgo 'Japanese language' + kyo⌐oiku 'education'/
    ni⌐hoNgokyo⌐oiku 'teaching Japanese as a foreign language'
ha⌐ru 'spring' + ya⌐sumi⌐ 'holiday'/ha⌐ruya⌐sumi 'spring
    vacation'

While there are various general principles which apply to words of different types, the distribution of accent patterns across Japanese words is certainly a complex topic, and the question arises of how much attention needs to be given to this matter by learners. Although the Tokyo-based system is accepted as standard, accentuation systems differ quite widely across Japanese dialects and regional varieties, so that the Japanese are accustomed to some variation in this aspect of the language; moreover, some words have variant patterns within the Tokyo system itself. Furthermore, though potentially high, the function of Japanese accentuation in distinguishing otherwise identical words (as in ka⌐ki vs ka⌐ki) is in practice often offset by context: pronouncing ka⌐ki ('persimmon') while clearly referring to an oyster will not generally lead to misunderstanding. Interestingly, accentuation is often ignored in the description of words in Japanese monolingual dictionaries. It has likewise often been neglected in teaching the language to foreign learners, and it is certainly absent from many textbooks and bilingual dictionaries. (Where it is dealt with, common alternatives to the bracket-style representation employed here include the placement of an acute accent on the accented mora—i.e. the last high mora before a drop in pitch—if present: thus, káki ('oyster'), kaki ('persimmon'), tabako, tamágo, arimásu, arimaséN.)

Nevertheless, this type of word accentuation remains a salient feature of most spoken varieties of Japanese, and the Tokyo system enjoys wide influence as the prestige norm. In the absence of contextual cues, confusion certainly does arise, and indeed accentuation may on occasion overrule distinctions in vowels and consonants: taᒻbako 'cigarette', for example, may be misheard as taᒻmaᒻgo 'egg' if mispronounced under the influence of the stress placement in English *tobacco*, and hiᒻtoᒻtu 'one' and huᒻtatu 'two' are a frequently confused pair. At the very least, learners should be aware of the broad characteristics of the standard system and, in particular, avoid the heavier patterns of English-style stress; ideally, it seems clear, they should learn words together with their standard accentual contours.

Illustration: Loanwords

A revealing way to highlight differences in the sound systems of different languages is to consider the pronunciation of loanwords. Loanwords—words 'borrowed' from one language into another—are filtered through the sound system of the borrowing language in the course of being adapted to their new surroundings.

English loanwords in Japanese

It is well known that Japanese has borrowed many words from English, and the sound shape of these loanwords bears the clear imprint of their Japanization. Perhaps the most notable difference between the sound systems of the two languages concerns syllable structure. As we have seen, Japanese permits syllables with at most one initial consonant, and syllable-final consonantal elements are restricted to N or the first part of a geminate k, s, t or p. English, by contrast, permits consonant clusters at both the beginning and the end of syllables—a one-syllable word such as *sprints* has the structure CCCVCCC. When borrowed, words of this kind become multi-syllable words in Japanese, with additional vowels being supplied to split up the original consonant clusters. Compare the following examples:

black → buᒻraᒻkku
spell → suᒻpeᒻru
glass → guᒻrasu

stress → *su̸⌈to⌉resu*
drive → *do⌈ra⌉ibu*
match → *ma⌉tti*

The general rule in such cases is to add the vowel *u* in Japanese, but *o* is usually added after original [t/d] (as in *stress/drive*) and *i* after original [tʃ/dʒ] (as in *match*). Another major difference is the greater repertoire of English sounds, and several pairs of English consonants (such as *r/l* and *b/v*) are rendered by a single sound in Japanese (in these cases, *r* and *b*). Note also that the placement of the accent may vary. In loanwords like *gu⌉rasu* and *su̸⌈to⌉resu*, the accent in Japanese falls on syllables which are not even present in the original English words. English names—both of places and of persons—must similarly be adapted to the Japanese sound system:

Australia → *o⌈osu̸tora⌉ria*
America → *a⌈merika*
Canberra → *kya⌈Nbera*
Sydney → *si⌉donii*
Melbourne → *me⌈rubo⌉ruN*
New York → *nyu⌈uyo⌉oku*
London → *ro⌉NdoN*
Smith → *su⌉misu*
Jones → *zyo⌈o⌉Nzu*
Lee → *ri⌉i*

Adaptation in borrowing is not always one-way; sometimes, the impact of a large influx of loanwords brings about changes in the sound system of the borrowing language. This has happened in the case of English loanwords in Japanese, which have given rise to new sound sequences not permitted in the traditional sound system. In the familiar syllable format, the most clearly established innovations are:

Ti (pronounced [ti])/*Di* ([di])
sye/zye/tye
fa/fi/fe/fo (*f* pronounced [ɸ])

In addition, a wider range of geminate consonants is permitted: *gg/zz/dd/bb/hh*. Compare the following loanwords illustrating these additional combinations:

> *party* → *paˡaTii*
> *disco* → *Diˡsɨko*
> *gesture* → *zyeˡsɨtyaa*
> *film* → *fiˡrumu*
> *bed* → *beˡddo*
> *staff* → *sɨˡˉtaˡhhu*

Japanese loanwords in English

Japanese names and other words borrowed into English undergo dramatic changes in vowel quality, including the loss of the important Japanese distinction between short and long vowels and, naturally, the loss of devoiced vowels. Equally noticeable are the related differences in the place and quality of accentuation; in the following examples, English stressed syllables are indicated by an acute accent:

> *yoˉkohama* → *Yokoháma*
> *toˉokyoo* → *Tókyo*
> *oˉosaka* → *Osáka*
> *naˡgoya* → *Nagóya*
> *taˉnaka* → *Tanáka*
> *kiˉmono* → *kimóno*
> *kaˉrate* → *karáte*
> *hɨˉtoN* → *fúton*
> *saˉke* → *sáke*
> *kaˉraoke* → *karaóke*

As indicated, English generally stresses the next-to-last syllable here (often with accompanying weakening of neighbouring unstressed vowels), but this is in most cases a rare position for the accented syllable in Japanese.

Connected speech

So far in this chapter we have focused on the pronunciation of single words in Japanese. In natural speech, however, words are not uttered one by one but strung together in phrases. Here too languages display their own characteristic sound patterns, with respect to phrasing and to the sound 'envelope' in which connected speech is packaged. These matters have been less studied and thus given less widespread attention in Japanese teaching materials, and they call for constructive listening to natural speech from the early stages of learning. The comments below are intended to highlight important features of phrase accentuation, prominence and intonation.

Phrase accentuation

By 'phrase' in this section we mean any sequence of words uttered together as one uninterrupted sound group. All languages string words together in this way in normal speech, with greater or lesser modifications in overall pronunciation.

How many phrases a given sequence of words—say, a sentence—will be broken into on a particular occasion of utterance depends on a variety of factors. Basically, phrasing involves the packaging of information into digestible chunks, and the way the speaker does this on any occasion will be influenced by the overall meaning of the sentence, his assessment of its impact on the hearer, situational factors such as noise, and so on. However, languages show certain patterns in this respect. In Japanese, the most important basic principle of phrasing is that a word and any following grammatical particles are normally pronounced as a single phrase:

> *SatoosaN-wa koko-ni imaseN-yo*
> 'Sato isn't here'

Here the grammatical particles *wa*, *ni* and *yo* are each pronounced together with the word which precedes them, as indicated by the hyphens. Most importantly, pauses naturally occur between phrases, rather than within them, so that any pauses—whether silent, or filled by hesitation noises or other elements—will occur after these particles. Language learners frequently need to hesitate, and it is important for English-speakers to learn to do so—when reading as well as speaking—after, rather than before, particles in this way.

Phrasing affects accentuation: within a single phrase, the basic accentual contours of individual words are smoothed into a single contour. The maximal division of the above sentence will be into three phrases:

Sa¯ˡtoosaN-wa/ koˈko-ni/ iˈmase¯ˡN-yo

Here the three phrases will each carry a single accentual contour as shown, the contour of each phrase resulting from the interaction of the accent patterns of its component words (in this case, the particles being all basically unaccented). Such a three-way division represents very careful speech; in most situations a two-way division or pronunciation as a single phrase will be much more natural:

Sa¯ˡtoosaN-wa/ koˈko-ni imaseN-yo
Sa¯ˡtoosaN-wa koko-ni imaseN-yo

In these cases the accentual contours will be modified. In general, as indicated, the first contour in each phrase predominates, with the remaining contours being smoothed (although not completely reduced) into a more level pattern. This smoothing of contours within phrases is the source of the standard advice to learners of Japanese, namely, when in doubt, to aim at a level contour.

Teaching materials do not always indicate these modified contours of connected speech directly. Accentuation is most commonly represented in the form of the basic contours for each individual word, and in connected sequences these need to be interpreted in the light of the normal adjustments discussed here. Clearly, a major function of accentuation in connected speech, in combination with the placement of pauses, is to indicate phrase divisions. These in turn reflect the chunking of information into manageable pieces, and major distortions in these areas will impair the overall comprehensibility of learners' spoken Japanese.

Prominence

It sometimes happens that we wish to highlight particularly important words in a spoken utterance. In Japanese this is done, once again, predominantly through pitch. Essentially, the accent contour of the word concerned is extended higher than it would be in normal circumstances. In the case of the sentence above, for example, we may wish to emphasize the fact that Sato, as opposed to other people, is not present, and this is done by raising the pitch of the accented syllable in $sa^\rceil toosaN\text{-}wa$, thus producing a wider pitch movement over the highlighted word. Again it is important to avoid the more dramatic effects of English-style stress, and to realize that the basic shape of the accent contour must be retained in Japanese. Thus in the following sentence:

> $Su^\lceil zukisaN\text{-}wa\ koko\text{-}ni\ imaseN\text{-}yo$
> 'Suzuki isn't here'

we may highlight $su^\lceil zukisaN\text{-}wa$ by again widening the pitch range; here, however, this will involve a higher rise from the first to the second syllable, and the basic low–high pattern must be preserved.

Intonation

Similar remarks apply to intonation in Japanese, i.e. to the pitch patterns associated with utterances indicating the speaker's intention, attitude, etc. The basic intonation patterns include falling and rising; the falling pattern generally indicating finality and commonly occurring in statements, the rising pattern indicating appeal to the hearer and commonly (though by no means invariably) occurring in questions. A third common intonation pattern, level, generally indicates incompleteness, as at the end of an unfinished sentence.

Once again, however, in Japanese these patterns are superimposed on the basic accentual framework, and this is apt to cause problems for English-speaking learners. Thus in Japanese informal speech, questions of the type in the following exchange are signalled purely by intonation:

> Q. $A^\rceil ru$?   A. $A^\rceil ru$.
> 'Are there any?'   'Yes, there are.'

In the question, the word *aru* is spoken with final rising intonation; however, this rise comes on the second syllable and follows the initial fall in pitch resulting from the basic accentual contour of the word. The tendency for English-speakers here is to spread the rising intonation over the whole word, overruling the contour. In the answer, by contrast, the accentual fall in pitch is followed by an intonational fall on the final syllable, giving an overall falling pitch throughout the word which comes naturally to English-speakers. In the following exchange, with an unaccented word, the opposite problem arises:

> Q. I⌐ru?   A. I⌐ru
> 'Is he/she there?'   'Yes, he/she is.'

Here the basic word-accentual contour is low–high, and the rising intonation in the question presents no difficulty. In the answer, however, the basic low–high contour must be retained, and the falling intonation on the second syllable is correspondingly inhibited; the temptation is to pronounce high–low in sympathy with the intonation, but *i⌐ru* is actually a distinct word (meaning 'roast').

Further study of these topics is needed, but it is clear that both prominence and intonation in Japanese are grafted onto the basic overall skeleton of accentual contours. Their operation is in this sense less dramatic than in English. It also seems that they play a smaller overall role in the language, in that what is achieved by these means in English is often achieved, or at least reinforced, by other means in Japanese. Thus contrast is often signalled by the use of the range particle *wa*, and intonation is often reinforced by illocutionary particles such as *ne*, *yo*, etc.

Precise description of these areas of pronunciation in writing is particularly difficult, and they can only be fully mastered on the basis of imitation. For this reason, in addition to familiarizing themselves with the basic facts, learners need to be exposed to natural connected speech from an early stage.

CHAPTER 3

WRITING

In our description of the sound system in chapter 2 we used the Roman alphabet to represent Japanese sounds and words. For some purposes this is an adequate representation; learners whose interests extend only to the spoken language, for example, can study Japanese through this medium, and many teaching materials are written in romanization. As the term implies, however, it remains an essentially alien transcription of the language, and learners with wider interests in Japanese must sooner or later come to grips with the native writing system.

Whatever its merits and intrinsic fascination, there can be no doubt that the Japanese writing system is the most complex in the world, and that its mastery requires an enormous investment of time and effort on the part of learners. This includes the Japanese themselves, who are still acquiring its finer details in the final years of secondary education. Unlike the Japanese, who come to the task with an established native command of the spoken language, English-speaking learners must master three unfamiliar scripts, ultimately comprising more than two thousand basic symbols, while still gaining competence in other areas of the language. The magnitude of this task accounts for the much greater time required to attain reading proficiency levels considered normal for languages with less complex writing systems. It also accounts for the higher proportion of teaching and learning time devoted to the mechanics of the writing system in general courses, inevitably at some cost to other important aspects of the language.

That said, large numbers of English-speaking learners succeed in mastering the system and becoming proficient readers of Japanese. Once again, while there is no substitute for the work of memorization and practice involved, the task is facilitated when based on a clear understanding of the structure of the system and of the principles of its use.

Scripts

The most notable feature of the Japanese writing system is that it employs a combination of several distinct scripts, as illustrated in the extract from a daily newspaper (figure 3.1). Moreover, the three central scripts—hiragana and katakana on the one hand, and kanji on the other—are based on quite different linguistic principles.

The vast majority of scripts in the world's languages are sound-based; the individual symbols of these scripts—like the letters of the English alphabet—relate to units of the sound system of the language concerned. This does not mean that all such scripts are 'phonetic' in the sense that they show an exact one-to-one correspondence with sound. The vagaries of English spelling, for example, are well known, and these are in many cases due to the conservatism of the writing system, which reflects features of pronunciation from an earlier stage of the language. Even in English, however, the broad sound–script correlations are clear, so that like-sounding words (such as *bank* ('financial institution') and *bank* ('of a river')) commonly share the same spelling. The English script is alphabetic; the basic relation is between symbols of the script and single vowel or consonant sounds. In Japanese, the kana scripts (hiragana and katakana) are also sound-based, but the basic relation is with moras rather than single vowels and consonants. Japanese moras, it will be recalled, take in short syllables (like *i*, *ko*, *zyu*) and lengthening elements (such as a lengthening vowel,

Figure 3.1 Extract from a Japanese daily newspaper

N, or the first half of a geminate *k/s/t/p*) and, broadly speaking, in the kana scripts each mora is written with a single symbol. Hiragana and katakana are sometimes referred to as 'syllabaries'; though adequate as a loose characterization, this is not strictly accurate since moras and syllables do not always coincide.

Much more rarely, scripts are based not on sound units but on units of the content plane of language. By this we refer to basic meaningful units such as English *house* or *boat*, which appear as simple words or as word components (as in compounds like *houseboat*). These units are known as 'morphemes', and scripts whose symbols relate to these units are morphemic scripts. The English writing system makes use of a few morphemic symbols, such as & ('and'), $ ('dollar'), etc, and numerals (1 'one', 7 'seven') are also basically morphemic, but in a truly morphemic script every morpheme is written with its own symbol. In this kind of script, items such as the two *bank*s will in principle be written with different symbols, since they have unrelated meanings and are thus different morphemes. Clearly, since there are far more distinct morphemes in a language than there are distinct sounds, morphemic scripts will contain a vastly greater number of symbols.

The prime examples of morphemic scripts in use today are Chinese characters and their borrowed counterparts in Korean (hanja) and Japanese (kanji). Once again, these scripts are not always described correctly, often being labelled as 'ideographic', which suggests that the symbols relate to ideas or concepts rather than to units of language. 'Logographic', implying a relation to *words*, is better but still not entirely accurate since, as we have seen, a compound word like *houseboat* will be written with two symbols, representing the *morphemes house* and *boat*.

In addition to hiragana, katakana and kanji, the modern Japanese writing system employs Arabic (and Roman) numerals, as well as the Roman alphabet. Below we look at these individual scripts in more detail and consider how they are combined in the overall system.

Hiragana

This is normally the first script acquired by foreign learners of the language (and by Japanese children). As we have seen, both hiragana and katakana are sound-based scripts that relate to moras rather than to single vowels and consonants. The first script known to the Japanese was the Chinese character script, and the kana scripts were developed in Japan by simplifying the shapes of certain characters which were conventionally used to represent the sounds of Japanese words. Their development reflects the relatively simple syllable structure of the language; Japanese syllables are composed of a limited number of mora shapes (just over a hundred), and to that extent a mora-based script is a practical medium in which to write the language.

Each kana script is built on forty-six basic symbols. The basic hiragana symbols, arranged in the conventional order, are shown in table 3.1.

Table 3.1 The basic hiragana symbols

あ *a*	い *i*	う *u*	え *e*	お *o*
か *ka*	き *ki*	く *ku*	け *ke*	こ *ko*
さ *sa*	し *si*	す *su*	せ *se*	そ *so*
た *ta*	ち *ti*	つ *tu*	て *te*	と *to*
な *na*	に *ni*	ぬ *nu*	ね *ne*	の *no*
は *ha*	ひ *hi*	ふ *hu*	へ *he*	ほ *ho*
ま *ma*	み *mi*	む *mu*	め *me*	も *mo*
や *ya*		ゆ *yu*		よ *yo*
ら *ra*	り *ri*	る *ru*	れ *re*	ろ *ro*
わ *wa*				を *(w)o*
ん *N*				

Remaining mora-shapes are written with the aid of two diacritics and of reduced forms of four of the basic symbols:

1 Moras with initial *g/z/d/b* are written with the symbols for

the corresponding moras with initial *k/s/t/h*, with the diacritic ˝ added. Thus, *ga* is written as *ka* plus ˝ (が), *sa* as *za* plus ˝ (ざ), etc.

2 Moras with initial *p* are written with the symbols for the corresponding moras with initial *h*, with the diacritic ° added: *pa* is written as *ha* plus ° (ぱ), etc.

3 Moras of the shape C*y*V (*kya*, etc.) are written with the symbol from the relevant *i* column (*ki*, etc.) followed by a small *ya/yu/yo* symbol. Thus, *kya* is written as *ki* plus small *ya* (きゃ), *gyu* as *gi* plus small *yu* (ぎゅ), etc.

4 The first part of a geminate *kk/ss/tt/pp* is represented by the symbol for *tu* written small (っ). Thus *sakki* (さっき), *assari* (あっさり), etc. (Note that *N* is always written as ん even in *Nn* and *Nm*, pronounced respectively as long *n* and *m*.)

Learners need to memorize the arrangement of the basic symbols as shown in table 3.1 (*a-i-u-e-o, ka-ki-ku-ke-ko*, etc.); the vertical sequence may be memorized as *a-ka-sa-ta-na, ha-ma-ya-ra-wa*. The arrangement (known as gojuuon 'fifty sounds', and applying to both kana scripts) corresponds to alphabetical order in English, and is the basis for the ordering of words in monolingual Japanese dictionaries and of names in lists. Note that, in this ordering, sounds written with diacritics come under the basic symbol concerned: words beginning with *ga* are listed under *ka*, words beginning with *ba* and *pa* under *ha*, words beginning with *kya* under *kiya*, and so on.

Since modern Japanese is written with a mixture of scripts, it is essential to understand the division of labour between them. Hiragana is generally used, firstly, to write grammatical elements. These include the inflectional endings of verbs and *i* adjectives (this use is known as okurigana); particles of various kinds; demonstrative words (e.g. *kore* 'this thing', *kono* 'this', *koo* 'in this way'); the copula (the verb 'to be': *da/desu*, etc.) and grammatical nouns such as *koto, no*, etc. Certain very general words that have both grammatical and non-grammatical uses are also normally written in hiragana, including common verbs like *aru* 'be located (of inanimates)', *iru* 'be located (of animates, etc.)', *suru* 'do', *naru* 'become' and the adjective *ii* 'good, OK'. Many (non-inflectional) affixes are written in hiragana, including the so-called 'honorific' prefix *o-* and many common suffixes. So are many adverbs (e.g. *totemo* 'very', *aNmari* '(not) much, (not) very'), including a large number of imitative items illustrated by *perapera* 'fluently', *bissyori* 'soakingly', *pokiN to* 'with a snap', etc. Items written in hiragana are generally native Japanese elements, but it is also used for Sino–Japanese items (i.e. items historically borrowed from classical Chinese) where kanji are not available; this happens mainly where the kanji involved have been pro-scribed from general use, as with the word *aisatu* 'greeting', formerly written with two kanji but now officially written in hiragana.

A major reform of kana spelling was carried out in 1946, as a result of which the scripts are now largely 'phonetic', i.e. in close correspondence with sound units. The main excep-tions affect hiragana:

1 The range particle *wa* is written with the symbol for *ha* (は), and the case particle *e* 'to' with the symbol for *he* (へ). What is historically the symbol for *wo* (を) is used uniquely to represent the case particle *o*.

2 The form *yuu* 'say, be called' is written as いう (*iu*).

3 The long vowel *oo* is generally represented as *ou*. However, it is written as *oo* in the stems of certain native Japanese items; these include *ookii* 'big', *ooi* 'numerous', *tooi* 'far', *tooru* 'go through/along', *kooru* 'freeze', etc.

4 The long vowel *ee* occurs predominantly in Sino–Japanese items, where it is represented in kana spelling as *ei*. How-ever, it is written as *ee* in a small number of native items, including the responder *ee*, the lengthened variant of the confirmatory particle *nee* and *oneesaN* 'elder sister'.

5 *zi/zu/zya/zyu/zyo* are spelt in two ways. The general spell-ing is as *si/su*, etc. with the diacritic ″ added (じ, ず). The alternative spelling is as *ti/tu*, etc. with ″ (ぢ, づ), used where these sounds are viewed as stemming from *ti/tu*: this occurs in words like *tizimeru* 'shorten' and *tuzuku* 'continue', in-

volving repetition in successive moras, and in compound words like *gohaNzyawaN* 'rice bowl', formed from *gohaN* 'boiled rice' plus *tyawaN* 'cup, bowl'.

Most of the exceptions listed under 3, 4 and 5 are in fact written with kanji in the normal orthography; however, knowledge of the correct kana spellings is necessary, for example, to locate these items in Japanese dictionaries. Note also that, in the reverse direction, i.e. going from writing to sound, the *spellings ou* and *ei* are ambiguous. While they commonly represent the sounds *oo* and *ee*, they may on occasion represent the sounds *ou* (as in verb forms like *omou* 'think') and *ei* (as in *ei* 'ray (fish)' and verb forms like *maneita* 'invited'), respectively.

Katakana

The basic katakana symbols are shown in table 3.2.

Table 3.2 The basic katakana symbols

ア *a*	イ *i*	ウ *u*	エ *e*	オ *o*
カ *ka*	キ *ki*	ク *ku*	ケ *ke*	コ *ko*
サ *sa*	シ *si*	ス *su*	セ *se*	ソ *so*
タ *ta*	チ *ti*	ツ *tu*	テ *te*	ト *to*
ナ *na*	ニ *ni*	ヌ *nu*	ネ *ne*	ノ *no*
ハ *ha*	ヒ *hi*	フ *hu*	ヘ *he*	ホ *ho*
マ *ma*	ミ *mi*	ム *mu*	メ *me*	モ *mo*
ヤ *ya*		ユ *yu*		ヨ *yo*
ラ *ra*	リ *ri*	ル *ru*	レ *re*	ロ *ro*
ワ *wa*				ヲ *(w)o*
ン N				

There are several formal similarities with hiragana (cf. *u*, *ka*, *se*, *he*, *mo*, *ya*, *ri*, etc.), reflecting the fact that the hiragana and katakana symbols were often derived from the same kanji; whereas hiragana developed as cursive abbreviations of whole kanji, katakana involved the use of selected components from their basic form, and this accounts for their stiffer, more angular appearance.

Extension of the basic symbols to the representation of other mora shapes works in essentially the same way as for hiragana. However katakana has a special vowel-length symbol (−), used to represent the second element of a long vowel: the word *baa* 'bar' is written バ−, etc. Exceptionally, the word *baree* 'ballet' is written バレエ, in contradistinction to *baree(booru)* 'volleyball' (バレ−).

The place of katakana in the overall writing system of modern Japanese is often compared to that of italics in printed English, i.e. it is used for items which are in some ways unusual or for some particular special effect. Thus its primary use is in representing loanwords other than from classical Chinese, notably from English and other European languages. As we have seen, these loanwords have resulted in additions to the traditional Japanese sound system in the form of new mora shapes such as *Ti, fa*, etc, and the conventions of the katakana script have also been extended to accommodate their written representation. The following spellings are clearly established:

Ti ティ *Di* ディ
sye シェ *zye* ジェ *tye* チェ
fa ファ *fi* フィ *fe* フェ *fo* フォ

As shown, these combinations involve the use of small forms of basic vowel symbols, with regular symbols indicating the initial consonant sounds. Katakana is also used in rendering foreign names; however, Chinese and Korean personal names written in characters in their original language are normally written in kanji. Elsewhere, katakana is regularly used to represent sound-imitative words (e.g. *kaakaa* (cawing sound), *riNriN* (ringing sound), *gatyaN* (crashing sound)), and exclamations and slang terms are also frequently highlighted by being written in katakana. A further use is to write the names of plants and animals where kanji are not available; as in other uses this results in improved readability by avoiding long sequences of hiragana.

While katakana is generally learned after hiragana, some materials for English-speaking learners introduce katakana first in view of its role in writing English names and loanwords. It goes without saying that, for both scripts, writing the symbols is an essential step in internalizing them. They should be written in the 'correct' way—i.e. with the correct number of strokes, in the correct order, each stroke in the correct direction (a stroke being any line written continuously, without lifting the pen). Careful attention needs to be paid to differentiating symbols of similar shape, such as katakana N (ン) and so (ソ), and si (シ) and tu (ツ), which differ in the direction of their component strokes. Symbols should also be roughly the same size, occupying the same proportion of a (real or imaginary) square. Full details of these matters are described in teaching manuals and reference works.

Kanji

The modern kanji script is the Japanized version of the Chinese character script, first encountered by the Japanese some 1500 years ago. While testifying to the cultural debt owed to China as the ultimate source of writing in Japan, the script has also undergone significant modifications in the course of its adaptation to Japanese, and we shall continue to distinguish between (Chinese) 'characters' and (Japanese) 'kanji'

Development of characters

The character script appears to have been developed as a morphemic script for Chinese more than 3000 years ago. Characters were devised to represent morphemes according to two major principles: semantic and phonetic/semantic. The semantic principle essentially involved direct representation of the meaning of the morpheme, either concrete or abstract: examples include 木 'tree', 一 'one', 中 'interior', 森 'forest' (i.e. a collection of trees), etc. The number of meanings that can be practically represented in this way is clearly limited, and the vast majority (close to 90%) of Chinese characters were formed on the phonetic/semantic principle. These characters contain two components, one (the 'phonetic') indicating the sound of the morpheme, the other (commonly called the 'radical') indicating its area of meaning. Thus, given the need to devise a character representing the morpheme 'mosquito' (pronounced *wén* in modern Mandarin), this may be effected by combining the character 虫 (*chóng* 'insect') and 文 (*wén* 'pattern, writing, etc'), as radical and phonetic respectively, in the new character 蚊 (i.e. 'an insect pronounced *wén*'). Naturally, the pronunciations relevant to the period when this character was formed are those of ancient Chinese rather than modern Mandarin, but the example clearly illustrates the basic principle, which is of major importance in the development of the character script. The majority of characters are thus constructed from recurrent formal components which often occur as characters in their own right. The pronunciation of the associated morpheme (*wén* in the case of 蚊) is said to constitute the 'reading' of the character concerned; in Chinese, a character normally represents a single morpheme and thus has a single reading.

Adaptation to Japanese

Chinese characters were the first form of writing introduced to Japan and, as well as learning to read and write Chinese, the Japanese set about adapting the script to write their own language. In this they faced certain difficulties based on the different grammatical structures of the two languages. In particular, whereas Chinese is an uninflected language, Japanese has both inflections and a large number of grammatical particles. Characters were ill-suited to representing elements of this kind, and the Japanese solution was to use them purely phonetically for these items, as if they were symbols from a sound-based script. That is, certain characters were used conventionally to represent Japanese *sounds* in such cases, based on their pronunciation in Chinese. Thus, the mora *ru* in Japanese was conventionally represented phonetically by characters such as 留 and 流 (both pronounced *liú* in Mandarin), quite independently of the meaning of their associated morphemes ('stop, remain' and 'flow' respectively). Over time, this use gave rise to the kana syllabaries (hiragana and katakana *ru* (る and ル) are simplified versions of the above characters), and in the modern Japanese writing system the phonetic use of kanji is restricted largely to certain names.

Elsewhere, the Japanese employed characters morphemically, but in two distinct ways. In the first place, as well as borrowing the Chinese script, the Japanese also borrowed vast numbers of Chinese words, much as English has borrowed from the European classical languages, Latin and Greek. These loanwords were pronounced in a Japanized approximation of Chinese, and they were written, naturally enough, with their normal characters. Thus, the Chinese morpheme for 'water' (pronounced *shuǐ* in modern Mandarin) was borrowed as *sui* and written with its regular character 水. From the viewpoint of the kanji, 水 has the Sino-Japanese reading (or 'on-reading', to use the familiar term) *sui*. At the same time, the Japanese took the important further step of extending the use of characters to represent native Japanese morphemes as well. In this case, 水 was also used to represent the native morpheme *mizu* '(cold) water', which thus constitutes the native Japanese reading (or 'kun-reading') of this kanji. In this way, unlike characters in Chinese, Japanese kanji typically acquired two readings, one Sino-Japanese and one native, normally with closely related meanings.

Some kanji acquired even more readings. Japanese borrowings from Chinese extended over many centuries and involved different regional varieties of the language; a morpheme borrowed once was often 'reborrowed' at a later stage with a different Sino-Japanese pronunciation reflecting its distinct pronunciation in the new variety. Thus, the kanji 木 has two on-readings: *boku* (the earlier reading) and *moku* (cf. modern Mandarin *mù*), as well as the kun-reading *ki*. Many kanji also have more than one kun-reading, as a result of having been associated with several native Japanese morphemes. While the various readings of a single kanji are generally closely related in meaning, in some cases they diverge widely. Thus the kanji 足 is used to write the noun *asi* 'foot, leg' as well as the verbs *tariru* 'be sufficient' and *tasu* 'add, supplement' (all native Japanese items), while its on-reading *soku* occurs with all these meanings. This is perhaps the place to point out that the 'meaning of a kanji' is often a somewhat vague notion. Kanji represent morphemes (i.e. readings), and strictly speaking it is morphemes which have meanings; the 'meaning of a kanji' amounts to no more and no less than the meanings of the various morphemes which it represents.

Unlike Chinese characters, then, Japanese kanji typically come with more than one reading. This is not always the case. While virtually all kanji have on-readings (the exceptions are kokuji, i.e. kanji devised in Japan such as 枠 *waku* 'frame' and 畑 *hatake* '(dry) field'), not all have kun-readings, and in fact about a third of the kanji in general use have a single, on-reading. However, a further third have one on- and one kun-reading, and a slightly smaller number have three or more readings. As an extreme example, the kanji 生 has twelve readings (two on and ten kun): native items written with 生 include *ikiru* 'live (vs die)'/*umu* 'give birth to'/*haeru* '(plants, hair, etc.) grow'/*nama* 'raw'. The vagueness of any single 'kanji-meaning' is particularly clear in cases of this kind.

A major feature of morphemic scripts is the large number of distinct symbols that they require. By typically associating one kanji with more than one morpheme, Japanese has achieved some economy in this respect, but even so recent surveys indicate that 4000–5000 kanji are in current use. Reform of the writing system has been a concern of the Japanese Government throughout this century, and various official recommendations have been made restricting the number of kanji approved for official use, as well as simplifying the form of some kanji and reducing the number of recognized readings. Currently 1945 kanji are sanctioned as 'general use kanji' (jooyookanji), of which 1006 must be learned in the first six years of compulsory schooling, i.e. during Japanese primary school education. A further 284 kanji are authorized for use in personal names. These recommendations apply only to government publications, education and the mass media, and kanji usage in various specialist fields as well as in literature accounts for the larger total given above.

To sum up, each Japanese kanji has a form—often composed of recurrent components—and one or more readings, i.e. associated morphemes, either native or Sino-Japanese, written with the kanji concerned. These morphemes, in turn, have meanings. In general, morphemes written with a single kanji are (more or less closely) related in meaning, but this is not invariably the case.

Function of kanji

Kanji are used to write all lexical (vs grammatical) words in modern Japanese, apart from the exceptions we have mentioned, notably imitative and some other, mainly native, words (written in hiragana) and loanwords and names chiefly from European languages (written in katakana). The division of labour between hiragana and kanji is well illustrated by words which have both grammatical and lexical uses and are distinguished in writing accordingly. A verb such as *miru*, for example, is written with kanji (見る) in the lexical meaning 'look at, see', but in hiragana (みる) when it functions as an auxiliary verb meaning '(do and) see, try (doing)'. This is an important point; learners often tend to overuse kanji in such cases, thereby transgressing a basic functional principle of the system. The example of *miru* also reminds us that (lexical) inflected words—i.e. verbs and *i* adjectives—are written in a combination of kanji and hiragana. The general principle here is that kanji represent the unchanging stems of such words and hiragana the inflectional endings, but in practice the situation is often more complicated. In the first place, the okurigana often takes in part of the stem due to its nature as a mora-based script; thus the invariable portion of the verb *hanasu* 'talk' is *hanas-*, but it is the final mora of the word, namely *su*, which is written in hiragana (話す). Beyond these script-induced cases, the hiragana section of many words by convention extends into the stem: many *i* adjectives, for example, have stems ending in *-si-*, and this is always written in hiragana together with the inflection: e.g. *kuwasii* 'detailed' (詳しい). Many uninflected words (including words derived from verbs and *i* adjectives, but not restricted to these) are also written partly in hiragana; the noun *usiro* 'place behind', for example, is written 後ろ, thereby avoiding confusion with *ato* 'time after' (後). It should also be noted that, while prescriptions for okurigana are given in government reforms, these do allow for some variation.

Kanji are of course generally used for Japanese personal names (although some given names are written in hiragana). As in most languages, the spelling of names in Japanese often involves additional complexities, notably a larger repertoire of prescribed kanji and, in many cases, an extended range of authorized readings. As noted earlier, Chinese and Korean personal names written in characters are also written in kanji, pronounced as regular on-readings: Zhou Enlai (周恩来) and Mao Zedong (毛沢東) are known as *syuu oNrai* and *moo takutoo* in Japanese. By contrast, the names of foreigners of Japanese descent are written in katakana: Mr Hayashi's surname will be written in kanji (林) if he is a Japanese national, but in katakana (ハヤシ) if he is, for example, a Japanese-American.

The normal use of the kanji script rests on the principle of one kanji per morpheme. Two marginal uses are found (generally called ateji 'assigned kanji') that infringe this principle. The first is the phonetic use of kanji alluded to earlier, where kanji are used essentially as sound-based symbols (in pronunciations close to, or identical with, their standard on-readings); this use is often found in names, as in place names like Nara (奈良) and Sasebo (佐世保). In the second, semantic use two or more kanji are assigned to write a single morpheme on the basis of meaning; thus the morpheme *otona* 'adult' is conventionally written with the two kanji 大人 ('big' + 'person') and the morpheme *inaka* 'country (vs town)' with the kanji 田舎 ('rice-field' + 'building').

Learning kanji

As with the kana symbols, mastery of the form of kanji can only be attained by writing them. While kanji often contain recurrent components, each component is in turn composed of a number of strokes; the ability to write a component correctly requires knowledge of the basic strokes and of the correct stroke order. (Ability to count strokes is also needed to use kanji dictionaries, which arrange kanji according to the stroke count of their components.) There is a limited repertoire of basic strokes (among which some 'bent' elements, such as 乙, are written continuously as single strokes), together with a series of principles governing stroke order, and once again these issues are fully treated in textbooks and reference works. A knowledge of common components, particularly of the more frequent radicals, is also helpful in learning kanji and in using dictionaries. Both radicals and phonetics are of varying reliability as indicators of general areas of meaning or of pronunciation. We have seen that the 'meaning of a kanji' is in any case an often vague notion, and the phonetics were, after all, based originally on ancient Chinese pronunciations rather than on those of modern Japanese. The components nevertheless retain importance as formal building-blocks, and the Japanese names of familiar radicals (such as *saNzui* 'water radical', *kiheN* 'tree radical', *kusakaNmuri* 'grass radical', etc.) are frequently used when identifying kanji in speech. When used as components most kanji retain their basic shape, being merely reduced in size: cf. 材, where 木 appears as a radical. Some, however, become modified, sometimes severely: cf. 打 with the 'hand radical' on the left (basically 手), and 沖, where the left-hand component is the 'water radical' (basic 水).

Clearly, the presence of multiple readings for most kanji presents problems for foreign learner-readers. On meeting a particular kanji in a text, how is one to know which reading to select? This is basically a vocabulary problem. A Japanese reader, who already has an extensive command of the vocabulary of the language, will select the vocabulary item which makes sense in the context, but foreign learners are typically required to read in advance of their vocabulary level. The clearest tendency—and it is no more than that—is that a single kanji standing alone (i.e. surrounded by kana) should be read in the kun-reading. This stems from the fact that Sino-Japanese morphemes tend to occur as word components rather than as single words in their own right. Thus the kanji 木 standing alone will be read *ki* ('tree', 'wood') rather than as *boku* or *moku*, which only occur in composite words such as *taiboku* 'enormous tree' and *mokuzai* 'timber' (each written with two kanji). A sequence of two kanji will generally be read both in the on-readings (as in these examples: 大木 *taiboku* and 木材 *mokuzai*) or, less commonly, both in the kun-readings (as in 植木 *ueki* '(pot-)plant'). Needless to say, exceptions to both principles occur. Some Sino-Japanese morphemes are used as independent words (e.g. *kiN* (金) 'gold'), and composite words occasionally mix on- and kun- readings (e.g. *nimotu* (荷物) 'luggage').

Finally, no account of the learning of kanji would be complete without reference to kanji dictionaries. Ordinary Japanese dictionaries list words in gojuuon order in kana spellings and thus provide information on words whose pronunciation is known. In Japanese, however, there is clearly a need for a further kind of dictionary that will enable the user to look up an unfamiliar kanji, whose pronunciation is unknown, encountered in reading. Monolingual dictionaries of this type, designed for Japanese users, are known as kanwajiten 'kanji–Japanese dictionaries'. The major requirement of such a dictionary is a coherent principle for the arrangement of kanji, and this is provided by stroke count. Firstly, all kanji are assigned to a particular radical, i.e. the component (in some cases the whole kanji) which is regarded as indicating, however vaguely, its broad area of meaning. Kanji such as 話 ('talk') and 語 ('word', 'language') are assigned to the radical 言, which also occurs as a kanji in its own right ('say'). Based on Chinese lexicographical practice, 214 radicals are normally recognized, and these are ordered in a fixed sequence on the basis of their stroke count. For example, 言 is a seven-stroke radical, which occurs as number 149 in the series. Individual kanji are then listed under each radical according to their total stroke count.

For example, 話 contains six strokes in addition to the radical and will therefore be listed before 語, which has seven additional strokes. Once located, the entry gives the on- and kun-readings of the kanji, together with information on meaning and a list of composite words in which the kanji appears. Kanji dictionaries normally also contain an index of readings (whereby a kanji whose on-reading is unknown, for example, can be located via a known kun-reading), and a total-stroke index (whereby a kanji whose radical is unclear can be located—somewhat laboriously—on the basis of its total stroke count).

The ability to use kanji dictionaries—and, hence, the ability to count strokes correctly—is an absolute necessity for learners of written Japanese. Fortunately, English-speaking learners are particularly well served in this respect, with several excellent bilingual Japanese–English kanji manuals and dictionaries (kan'eijiten 'kanji–English dictionaries') now available. These generally incorporate improved schemes—explained in each of the individual works—for ascertaining the radical of a kanji on the basis of its formal patterning rather than on the basis of meaning, a major difficulty with the traditional system. Readings are given in romanization (on-readings in capitals, kun-readings in lower case, with okurigana sections given in brackets), as are important composite words in which the kanji appears, together with other useful information. Instruction and training in the use of these dictionaries are indispensable elements of any written Japanese course.

The complexities of the kanji script are considerable, and its mastery adds a major dimension to the learning of Japanese. Since the learning of kanji is inevitably a partial exercise (even the Japanese occasionally encounter kanji, or readings of kanji, with which they are not familiar), it seems important—particularly in the earlier stages—to tie their acquisition to known vocabulary; the general strategy here will be to learn to read kanji used to write known vocabulary and to master the principles of the script (together with the mechanics of using kanji dictionaries) so as to permit individual progress at more advanced levels. This applies to individual readings as well as to kanji themselves; while kanji are often programmed to be learned as items, with their full complement of readings, different readings often vary widely in their frequency as vocabulary items. From a 'vocabulary first' perspective, there is no reason why all readings should be acquired simultaneously.

Other scripts

While the kanji and kana scripts, stemming ultimately from Chinese characters, are at the heart of the Japanese writing system, they are not the only scripts used to write the language. Modern written Japanese is further enlivened by the presence of additional symbols originating in Western languages, namely Roman letters and Arabic and Roman numerals.

Letters of the Roman alphabet, chiefly capitals, are regularly used in a variety of abbreviations and acronyms, commonly based on English and thus constituting a special group of loanwords. It is important to realize that such items are fully-fledged members of the Japanese vocabulary and so should be distinguished from genuine English words, in English spelling, used as brand-names, advertising slogans, etc. Examples obviously borrowed from English include PR (pronounced *piiaaru*), FM (*ehuemu*), SF (*esuehu*). Others have been coined in Japan on the basis of English words (e.g. OL (*ooeru*) 'office lady, i.e. young female office worker', SL (*esueru*) 'steam locomotive', JR (*zyeeaaru*) 'Japan Railway'), or in some cases on the basis of Japanese, as in NHK (*enuettikee*), based on the initial letters of *nippoN hoosoo kyookai* 'Japanese Broadcasting Corporation'. Initials in foreign personal names are also written in Roman capitals: John D. Smith is written ジョン・D・スミス (*zyoN Dii sumisu*). Metric units, also commonly written in Roman letters, use lower case as well as capitals: 50 mm (pronounced *gozyuumiri*), 4 ℓ (*yoNrittoru*), 100 kg (*hyakukiro-(guramu)*), 300 kW (*saNbyakukirowatto*), etc.

As the previous examples make clear, Arabic numerals (*arabiasuuji*) are also widely used in modern Japanese. The kanji script has its own numerals (known as kansuuji) (一 (1), 二 (2), 三 (3), 十 (10), 百 (100), etc.), but their use as true numerals is largely restricted to traditional vertical writing. Two systems are found in writing these: a 'long' system with place-indicating numerals included (e.g. 231 written 二百三十一, i.e. 'two hundred and thirty-one') and a 'short' system as used generally with Arabic numerals (二三一, i.e. 'two three one'); in the latter system zero is written with the symbol ○ (二○一 '201'). In horizontal writing Arabic numerals are the rule, and they are frequently encountered in vertical writing as well. Finally, Roman numerals (I, II, III, etc.) are commonly employed to number chapters or sections in books.

With the exception of Roman numerals, the multiple scripts of Japanese may occur in various combinations in the representation of a single word. Mixtures of kanji and hiragana are commonplace, as in inflected words like *miru* (見 る). Other combinations are exemplified in the following: 歯ブラシ *haburasi* 'toothbrush', おトイレ *otoire* 'toilet', B面 *biimeN* 'B-side (of record)', LP ガス *erupiigasu* 'LP gas', 2DK *niiDiikee* '(apartment) consisting of two rooms plus a dining room-cum-kitchen', イギリス人らしい *igirisuziNrasii* 'typical of the English'.

Punctuation

Punctuation conventions, including the repertoire of punctuation marks or symbols themselves, are an important component of writing systems. We therefore end this section with some brief comments on Japanese punctuation.

Perhaps the most striking general contrast with written English in this area is the lack of word spacing in Japanese. There is also no distinction corresponding to capitals vs lower case in English. Where they occur, comma- and period-type punctuation marks naturally indicate phrase and sentence divisions, but within these units the symbols of the various scripts follow each other without breaks.

Basic Japanese punctuation marks include 、 and 。 , which correspond broadly to the comma and fullstop, respectively;

a third element, the raised dot (·) functions to separate closely linked elements of the same type and is used, for example, to punctuate foreign names (ジョン・スミス 'John Smith'). Quotation marks in Japanese generally take the form of square 'hooks' (「 」, also 『 』) rather than apostrophes. Other notable features include the wavy dash (〜) linking time or place expressions and indicating 'from ... to' (2時〜4時 'from 2:00 to 4:00'), and the kanji repetition symbol (々), used to indicate repetition of the preceding kanji in reduplicated words: 国々 kuniguni 'countries', etc.

Variations

The previous section has examined the core of the Japanese writing system, in particular the nature of the various scripts and the principles of their normal use. In real life, in fact we find a good deal of variation in the use of scripts. We must also consider the direction of writing—Japanese is written both vertically and horizontally—and formal differences between printed and handwritten styles.

Orthographic variation

The peculiar nature of the Japanese writing system obviously affords wide scope for variation in the written representation of the language. Thus, theoretically Japanese can be written entirely in kana. Indeed it is so written, for example, in books for young children (sometimes with a sprinkling of basic kanji). Paradoxically, Japanese written in this way is often difficult to read, and kana texts generally incorporate spacing (between phrases, rather than between single words) as an indication of meaningful divisions. Some beginning textbooks for foreign learners also use this device, but this is open to the criticism of being artificial unless the materials are specifically directed at children.

Leaving aside such special cases, considerable variation is found in the use of the scripts, especially of kanji, in everyday written Japanese. As we have seen, government prescriptions on the number and authorized readings of kanji are aimed at the official public sphere, and freer use of kanji is found in literature and in private writing. To ensure readability in such cases, unauthorized kanji in published materials are often accompanied by furigana, consisting of small hiragana symbols written over or alongside the kanji concerned, indicating the intended reading. (Furigana is also found with kanji proper names, which often have several possible readings.)

On the other hand, we also find kana where we might expect kanji. When writing, even the Japanese sometimes forget the correct 'spelling' of a kanji word, but avoidance of kanji may also result from indeterminacy in the system itself, as with some native words which are officially written with different kanji in different shades of meaning. The verb *toru* 'take', for example, is assigned five different kanji in 'take notes' (取る), 'take (on) an employee' (採る), 'take (up) one's pen' (執る), 'take (i.e. catch) a mouse' (捕る), and 'take a photo' (撮る). In a given context, the 'correct' choice among such alternatives may not always be clear, and the easiest solution for the writer is often to fall back on hiragana (とる).

Variation is also found between hiragana and katakana, notably in writing imitative items such as *gatyaN* 'with a crash', *bissyori* 'soakingly', etc. The general principle here is to use katakana only for sound-imitative words (like *gatyaN*), but in practice its use is often extended beyond these.

Vertical and horizontal writing

Variation is also found in the direction of Japanese writing. The modern language is written both vertically, beginning at the top right of the page and proceeding in columns to the left, and horizontally, as in English, proceeding from the top left. Which end of a Japanese book is the front thus depends on the format in which it is written.

Vertical writing (tategaki) is the traditional system and is still the norm for most published materials. Newspapers are basically vertical (although with some horizontal headlines and captions); however, numerical listings in newspapers— such as share prices and television and radio schedules—are in horizontal format, as are some advertisements. Horizontal writing (yokogaki) is particularly associated with scientific fields, where it is more suited to the incorporation of numerals and mathematical formulae. Books in other academic fields also appear in yokogaki, and some academic journals have both vertical and horizontal sections, beginning at opposite ends.

As we have seen, the direction of writing has some implications for the writing system, in that kanji numerals are found (as true numerals) only in vertical writing. There are also effects on punctuation with, for example, the English-style comma and full-stop sometimes replacing the Japanese ， and ○ in horizontal writing.

Script styles

As with all scripts, there are differences among the various printed and handwritten shapes of Japanese kanji and kana symbols. The central representative style for kanji is known as kaisho; this is a square handwritten style, which is the basis for stroke counts and the style normally taught first in textbooks and other teaching materials. Kaisho is close to printed styles, although the latter incorporate additional minor embellishments in certain strokes. Among more fluid handwritten styles we find gyoosho (semi-cursive) and soosho (cursive); while gyoosho shapes remain broadly recognizable (with practice), soosho involves dramatic formal modifications and is chiefly of interest to calligraphers.

Romanization

Romanization is the written representation of Japanese in the Roman alphabet. As such it is designed for foreign consumption and, not unnaturally, without practice ordinary Japanese find it difficult to read romanized Japanese texts.

The history of romanization goes back to the first contacts between Europeans and Japanese. In attempting to represent the sound of Japanese words in writing, foreigners naturally used the letters of their own alphabet and followed the spelling conventions of their own language. In this way various systems of romanization arose, reflecting such different European languages as Portuguese, Dutch, German, French and English. The best known of these European-based systems is undoubtedly the Hepburn system, employed by the American James Hepburn in the third edition of his Japanese–English dictionary, published in 1886. In addition, the Japanese themselves developed romanization systems, notably the Nipponshiki system in 1881 and the closely related Kunreishiki system in 1937 (slightly modified in 1954). The chief difference between Hepburn and these Japanese systems is in the representation of consonant sounds: the Hepburn system is concerned to indicate pronunciation according to English conventions (and thus spells *shi*, *chi*, *tsu*, etc.), whereas the Japanese systems aim to reflect the workings of the sound system independently of such considerations (thus *si*, *ti*, *tu*, etc.).

Textbooks and dictionaries for English-speaking learners generally adopt one or other of these systems, sometimes with additional modifications. Table 3.3 lists the main points of difference between the systems, together with other variations more or less commonly employed. Unlike the Japanese writing system, romanized Japanese generally employs word divisions, and minor variations in conventions are also found here.

Which of the systems, and the different variations, is best? The answer depends on the purpose for which they are used. For example, in writing about Japan directed at the general English-speaking reader (as opposed to the Japanese-language student), the Hepburn system has the advantage of indicating at least a phonetically closer approximation of Japanese pronunciation (as in Mt Fuji rather than Mt Huzi). (However, even the Hepburn system sometimes follows kana spelling, rather than pronunciation, notably in its use of the spellings *ei* (vs *ee*) and *iu* (vs *yuu*).) At the same time the Hepburn system distorts systematic relations among certain Japanese sounds, and this can be confusing for beginning language-learners. In verb inflection, for example, a pattern such as *matsu/machimasu/ matanai* is made to appear irregular in Hepburn, whereas its

Table 3.3 The major systems of romanization

	Hepburn	Kunreishiki (Nipponshiki)	Others
Long vowels	ā, ī/ii, ū, ē, ō	â, î, û, ê, ô	aa, ii, uu, ee, oo
えい (in Sino-Japanese items)	ei	ei	ee
が, etc (where optionally [ŋa])	ga	ga	ḡa
し	shi	si	
しゃ、しゅ、しょ	sha, shu, sho	sya, syu, syo	
じ	ji	zi	
じゃ、じゅ、じょ	ja, ju, jo	zya, zyu, zyo	
ち	chi	ti	ci
ちゃ、ちゅ、ちょ	cha, chu, cho	tya, tyu, tyo	cya, cyu, cyo
ぢ	ji	zi(di)	
ぢゃ、ぢゅ、ぢょ	ja, ju, jo	zya, zyu, zyo (dya, dyu, dyo)	
つ	tsu	tu	cu
づ	zu	zu(du)	
ふ	fu	hu	
を	o	o(wo)	
ん	n/n'/m	n/n'	ñ; N
っ	NB: t(ch)		t(c); c(c); Q
ティ	ti	t'i	t(e)i; Ti
ディ	di	di	d(e)i; d'i; Di
ファ、フィ、フェ、フォ	fa, fi, fe, fo	fa, fi, fe, fo	h(u)a, etc; hwa, etc.
いう	iu	iu	yuu

Kunreishiki version (*matu*/*matimasu*/*matanai*) shows it as completely parallel to the regular pattern in *kaku*/*kakimasu*/*kakanai*. In addition, some of the supplementary variations are to be preferred on pedagogical grounds. In particular, the important distinction between long and short vowels in Japanese is captured with more visual impact where long vowels are written double (*aa*, etc.) than where they are distinguished only by a superscript diacritic (*ā*, *â*, etc.). It also seems important to distinguish the syllable-final nasal from the consonant *n*, again preferably without the use of diacritics; as well as being more easily overlooked, diacritics are typographically inconvenient. Additional refinements mentioned in chapter 2 include the indication of devoicing (important in the early stages) and of word accentuation (highly desirable in word lists and dictionaries) and, less commonly, of phrase accentuation and other aspects of connected speech. Although we become attached to the romanization system we are most used to, the differences are relatively minor, and serious language students should make an effort to become familiar with the full range.

Finally, why should language-learners bother with romanization at all? Provided that their interest goes further than the spoken language, why not learn to read and write Japanese in kana from the very first? Certainly many teachers favour this approach, on the grounds that this is the more natural course, which makes the best use of the time available, avoids later transition problems and takes advantage of the inherent interest which an unfamiliar script holds for many students. Others believe strongly that it is pedagogically preferable to gain some initial footing in the pronunciation, grammar and vocabulary of the language unencumbered by this additional burden. They also point out that romanization permits the simpler statement of many inflectional rules. Once again, this is an area of strong allegiances. Whichever method is adopted in teaching the language, the fact remains that many excellent teaching and reference materials make use of romanization. If we are to avail ourselves of these in our study of Japanese, we need to control romanization—ultimately because it is there.

CHAPTER 4

VOCABULARY

Sound and writing systems belong to the expression plane of language. Essentially, they are formal mechanisms through which meanings are transmitted in speech and writing. The meanings themselves originate in the content plane of language, which consists of vocabulary and grammar.

Broadly speaking, vocabulary is the stock of words in a language and grammar the way in which these words are arranged, linked and formally modified in the construction of sentences. This will not quite do, since grammar often makes use of a set of words of its own ('grammatical words') that play important roles in building sentences; however, such words always form a limited, relatively small set, and the vast majority of words in a language ('lexical words') belong in the vocabulary. Japanese grammatical words ('particles', etc.), as well as the grammatical modification of words (inflection), will be dealt with in chapter 5; our concern here is with the immense stock of lexical words.

The crucial importance of vocabulary in both the comprehension and production of language is obvious, and it is a remarkable fact that native knowledge of any language involves the control of tens of thousands of words. The precise size of vocabularies is in fact impossible to determine, since they are open-ended in the sense that new terms are continually being added to meet new needs. The largest modern dictionary of Japanese (the Nihon Kokugo Daijiten) contains some 400,000 entries, a figure comparable to that of the *Oxford English Dictionary*, but of course vast numbers of these items are rarely encountered in everday life. Even so, it seems clear that a basic everyday vocabulary contains at least ten thousand words.

Learning the vocabulary of any foreign language thus involves a prodigious feat of memory. For the English-speaking learner of Japanese, the task is magnified by the general lack of formal resemblance between Japanese and English words. Whereas most European languages are genetically and culturally related to English and share a good deal of cognate vocabulary, in the case of Japanese the learner must set out from scratch in a totally unfamiliar landscape. (The only exception to this, of course, is provided by English loanwords.) In addition to formal shapes, words also have meanings. While vocabulary lists and dictionaries may sometimes give the impression that Japanese and English words can be equated in meaning on a one-to-one basis, this is in fact rarely the case. The vocabulary of a language is an index of the culture of its speakers; Japan's traditions and social organization are in many ways quite different from those of the English-speaking world, and these and other cultural differences are naturally reflected in the meanings of words. Mastery of Japanese semantics—i.e. the meanings of Japanese lexical and grammatical items— is one of the most difficult tasks facing the learner of the language.

Vast though vocabulary is, it is more than a simple agglomeration of isolated words. As in all languages, Japanese words are related in various ways, and the main purpose of this chapter is to explore the most important of these lexical groupings.

Word classes

The words of a language fall into groups according to the way they behave in sentences. These groups are known as 'word classes' or 'parts of speech'. The word classes recognized for a particular language are the product of analysis, and different scholars may divide them differently according to the weight they attach to different criteria. Here we divide the lexical words of Japanese into the four classes of noun, adjective, verb and adverb according to the features described below.

Nouns

The primary characteristic of nouns in Japanese is that they may appear in sentences (alone or modified) marked by the case particles *ga* or *o*. Thus the word *kuruma* 'car' is classified as a noun on the basis of sentences such as *Asuko ni kuruma ga tomatte iru* 'There is a car stopped over there' and *Atarasii kuruma o kaoo* 'Let's buy a new car'. In addition, nouns may be specified or modified by the demonstrative words *kono* 'this'/ *sono* 'that (near you)'/ *ano* 'that (over there)' (cf. *kono kuruma* 'this car'), by adjectives (cf. *hurui kuruma* 'old car', *kiree na kuruma* 'beautiful car') and by other nouns followed by the genitive case particle *no* (cf. *musume no kuruma* 'my daughter's car'). In terms of meaning, typical nouns denote concrete objects (like *kuruma*), persons (like *musume* 'daughter'), animals (cf. *inu* 'dog') and the like, but meaning does not serve directly as a basis for word-class assignment. A word such as *kaminari* 'thunder and lightning' denotes an event, but it is classified as a noun in view of its behaviour in sentences (*Kaminari ga natte iru* 'It's thundering', *yuube no kaminari* 'the thunder last night', etc.). Some grammarians define Japanese nouns much more widely than here, as taking in most non-inflected lexical words, but this downplays important differences in behaviour in sentences and results in a large proliferation of subclasses.

Japanese nouns are uninflected. In this they differ from English nouns, which inflect for number (singular vs plural: *car/cars*, *dog/dogs*, etc.). In Japanese, whether a noun refers to a single entity or to more than one is not normally indicated by the form of the noun. The phrase *hurui kuruma* will correspond sometimes to 'old car', sometimes to 'old cars'. Naturally, Japanese can make this distinction clear when necessary (by using numbers, quantity words like 'many', etc.); the point is that no obligatory formal distinction of this type is made in the noun itself. The only exception is found with nouns referring to specific individuals such as *watasi* 'I', *satoosaN* 'Sato', *okaasaN* 'Mother', etc; these have singular reference unless they are explicitly marked with a pluralizing suffix (cf. *watasitati* 'we', *satoosaNtati* 'Sato and his/her group', *okaasaNtati* 'Mother and her group'). Note that, while words like *I* are in English normally assigned to the distinct (grammatical) word class of pronouns, their separate status is much less clear in Japanese. In particular, whereas English personal pronouns form a small, closed class, their Japanese counterparts are more numerous. Common equivalents for *I*, for example, include *ore* and *boku* for male speakers, *atasi* for female speakers and *watasi* and *watakusi* for both sexes, the choice between these options being determined primarily on the basis of the social relationship between the speaker and the addressee. In use, words of this kind fall together with personal names and titles. Japanese counterparts of English *you* include *omae*, *kimi*, *aNta* and *anata*, but these are heavily restricted in use, and the most general way to refer to the addressee is by name (e.g. *satoosaN*) or by title (e.g. *okaasaN*, *seNsee* (used for teachers, doctors, etc.)).

Adjectives

Adjectives in Japanese are words that characteristically modify nouns or form predicates. Words like *hurui* 'old' and *kiree* 'beautiful, clean' are adjectives: cf. *hurui kuruma* 'old car'/ *kiree na kuruma* 'beautiful car', where these words modify the noun *kuruma*, and *Kono kuruma wa hurui* 'This car is old', *Kono kuruma wa kiree da* 'This car is beautiful', where they form predicates. Adjectives themselves are modified by adverbs: e.g. *sugoku hurui kuruma/sugoku kiree na kuruma* 'an awfully old/ beautiful car', where they are modified by the adverb *sugoku* 'awfully'. In terms of meaning, adjectives typically denote qualities or states.

Japanese adjectives fall into different formal groups. Adjectives like *hurui* are inflected. As well as *hurui* (non-past), this word has other forms such as *hurukatta* (past), *huruku* (-*ku* form), *hurukute* (conjunctive: 'and'-form), etc. Moreover, the non-past and past forms of these adjectives (*hurui, hurukatta*) may stand alone as predicates (corresponding to 'is old', 'was old'), as illustrated for *hurui* above. The non-past form of these inflected adjectives always ends in -*ai*, -*ii*, -*ui* or -*oi*, and they are commonly called '*i* adjectives'. Most of the basic Japanese adjective pairs belong here: *ookii* 'big'/*tiisai* 'small'; *ii* 'good'/ *warui* 'bad', *takai* 'expensive'/*yasui* 'cheap', *nagai* 'long'/*mizikai* 'short', *hiroi* 'spacious'/*semai* 'constricted', *hutoi* 'thick, fat'/ *hosoi* 'thin, slender', *atui* 'thick'/*usui* 'thin', *hurui* 'old'/*atarasii* 'new', etc. *Ooi* 'numerous, plentiful'/*sukunai* 'few, little' are a basic pair that occur as predicates rather than as modifiers: *Ame ga ooi* 'Rain is plentiful'/**ooi ame* 'plentiful rain'. As inflected words, *i* adjectives resemble Japanese verbs; however, *i* adjective inflections differ in shape and are less numerous than those of verbs. Also, unlike verbs, Japanese adjectives never govern nouns marked by the case particle *o*.

Other Japanese adjectives are uninflected; thus *kiree* never changes its basic shape, unlike *hurui*. Adjectives like *kiree* are linked to the nouns they modify by the form *na* and are thus often called '*na* adjectives'. Unlike *i* adjectives, *na* adjectives may not stand alone as predicates but must be combined with forms of the copula *da* (*kirei da* 'is beautiful', *kiree datta* 'was beautiful', etc.). In vocabulary lists for learners, it is useful to indicate these adjectives clearly, and we shall cite them as *kiree na*, etc. Other common *na* adjectives include *zyoozu na* 'skil-ful', *heta na* 'poor, unskilful', *geNki na* 'in good spirits', *heN na* 'odd, strange', *suki na* 'fond (of)', *kirai na* 'not fond (of)'. The *i* adjectives *ookii* 'big'/*tiisai* 'small' also often occur in the alternative forms *ooki na*/*tiisa na* when modifying nouns (*ookii kuruma*/*ooki na kuruma*, both 'big car'). Being uninflected, *na* adjectives are sometimes treated as a type of noun. However, these words are not followed by the case particles *ga* or *o*, and they are modified by adverbs rather than by adjectives. (It is worth noting that English, too, has inflected and unin-flected adjectives: e.g. *easy* (*easier*/*easiest*) vs *difficult* (**difficulter*/ **difficultest*).)

A further group of uninflected adjectives differs from *na* adjectives in being followed by the form *no* rather than *na* when they modify nouns: cf. *pikapika no kuruma* 'sparkling (clean) car'/*Kono kuruma wa pikapika da* 'This car is sparkling (clean)'. We shall refer to them as '*no* adjectives' and cite them accordingly: *pikapika no* 'sparkling (clean)', etc. Other exam-ples are *hadaka no* 'naked', *nama no* 'raw', *bisyobisyo no* 'soaking (wet)', *garagara no* 'deserted', *katikati no* 'rock hard', etc. Some adjectives alternate between *na* and *no*: *seesiki* 'formal', for example, appears in both *seesiki na syorui* and *seesiki no syorui* 'formal documents'; these adjectives may be cited as *seesiki na/no* 'formal', etc. Finally, the common adjective *onazi* 'same' is formally unique. It is uninflected and combines with the copula when used predicatively (*onazi da* 'is the same', etc.) but modifies nouns directly without any linking form (*onazi kuruma* 'the same car', etc.).

The distinctions between *i* adjectives, *na* adjectives and *no* adjectives are purely formal—like the difference between *easy* (inflected) and *difficult* (uninflected) in English. Irrespective of formal divisions like these, word classes also contain subclasses based, like word classes themselves, on behaviour in sentences. Subclasses show the major properties of the word class but with particular characteristics of their own. Japanese adjectives include an extremely important subclass of this kind, which we shall call 'subjective' adjectives. The characteristic feature of subjective adjectives is that they may be used, in simple declarative sentences, to describe a state experienced by the first person ('I'), but not by second or third persons ('you', 'he/she/they'). An example is the *i* adjective *uresii* 'happy, glad': in Japanese the sentence *(Watasi wa) uresii* 'I am glad' is grammatical, but **Anata wa uresii* 'You are glad' and **SatoosaN wa uresii* 'Sato is glad' are not. Other examples include *samui* 'cold (of overall bodily sensation)', *kayui* 'itchy', *itai* 'in pain', *kowai* 'afraid', *kanasii* 'sad', *zaNneN na* 'sorry, regretful' etc. Subjective adjectives describe sensory and emotional states and reactions; these are private states directly accessible only to the person who experiences them, and the restriction on their use is understandable on this basis. What is significant for learners is that English grammar does not operate in the same way; in English, *Sato is glad*, *Sato is cold*, etc. are grammatical sentences. To express these propositions in Japanese, one has to say things like 'Sato looks glad', 'Sato is showing signs of being glad', 'Sato says he is glad', etc, making explicit reference to the evidence on which they are based.

Verbs

Japanese verbs characteristically function as predicates: in the sentence *Atarasii kuruma o kaoo* 'Let's buy a new car', a form of the verb *kau* 'buy' occurs as predicate. Verbs are modified by adverbs: in *Kono kuruma wa yoku hasiru* 'This car runs well' the verb *hasiru* 'run' is modified by the adverb *yoku* 'well'. Semantically, typical verbs denote actions and events.

Like *i* adjectives, Japanese verbs are inflected: *kau* (non-past) has a variety of other forms such as *katta* (past), *katte* (conjunctive), *kaoo* (hortative: 'let's . . . '), *kawanai* (negative non-past), etc. Whereas the non-past form of *i* adjectives ends in -*i*, in Japanese verbs it ends in one of the following: -*au*, -*ou*, -*uu*, -*ku*, -*gu*, -*su*, -*tu*, -*nu* (only in the verb *sinu* 'die'), -*bu*, -*mu*, -*ru*. Verbs also have a wider range of forms than *i* adjectives (including imperatives: *kae* 'buy!' etc.), and combine with (grammatical) auxiliary verbs of various kinds (cf. *katte iru* 'be buying/have bought', *katte oku* 'buy for future use', *katte kureru* 'buy (for me, us, etc.)'). Unlike adjectives, many verbs (including *kau*) govern nouns marked by the case particle *o*.

Formally, Japanese verbs fall into two main inflectional groups (conjugations), with a handful of exceptions; details are given in chapter 5. Here we focus on three particularly important dimensions of verb subclassification, namely aspect, valency and volition.

In terms of aspect, Japanese verbs are either dynamic or stative. Dynamic verbs occur as predicates both in their basic form (*kau*, etc.) and in combination with the auxiliary verb *iru* (*katte iru*, etc.), whereas stative verbs occur in only one of these. Thus the verb *aru* 'be located (of inanimates)' does not combine with this auxiliary (**atte iru*) and is thereby shown to be a stative verb; similar verbs are *iru* 'be located (of animates)', *dekiru* 'be possible', *iru* 'be necessary', *nagasugiru* 'be too long'. Similarly, some verbs occur as predicates *only* in combination with *iru*, such as *sugurete iru* 'be outstanding, superior' (**sugureru*), *assarisite iru* 'be plain, simple' (**assarisuru*). Semantically, stative verbs denote states or qualities rather than actions or events.

The vast majority of Japanese verbs are dynamic. These fall into two broad semantic groups, denoting actions and changes of state, respectively. Action verbs are exemplified by *kau* 'buy', *taberu* 'eat', *suru* 'do', *asobu* 'play', *yomu* 'read', *huru* 'fall (e.g. of rain)', etc, and combinations of these with the auxiliary *iru* commonly refer to action in progress (*katte iru* 'be buying', *tabete iru* 'be eating', *hutte iru* '(rain) be falling', etc.). Examples of change-of-state verbs are *tomaru* '(come to a) stop', *tukareru* 'become tired', *naru* 'become', *naoru* 'become cured, repaired', *kowareru* 'become broken', *iku* 'go', *kuru* 'come'. Most importantly, in combination with *iru* these verbs refer not to action in progress but only to resultant state: *tomatte iru* 'be in the resultant state of having come to a stop, i.e. be stopped', *tukarete iru* 'be tired', *itte iru* (from *iku* 'go') 'be (at a place, having gone there)', etc. Change-of-state verbs are intransitive (i.e. they do not govern a central noun marked by the case particle *o*), but they frequently have transitive partners, denoting an action which brings about the change concerned: cf. *tomaru* '(come to a) stop'/*tomeru* '(bring to a) stop', *naoru* 'become cured, repaired'/*naosu* 'cure, repair', *kowareru* 'become broken'/*kowasu* 'break (something)'. As shown by these examples, such intransitive/transitive pairs are generally formally related. They also illustrate the important fact that, unlike English, Japanese generally keeps intransitive and transitive verbs apart. Whereas the English verb *stop* is used both intransitively (*The car stopped*) and transitively (*He stopped the car*), Japanese has the pair of distinct, though related, verbs *tomaru*/*tomeru*. Similar examples (intransitives first) include *begin*/*hazimaru* ~ *hazimeru*, *open*/*aku* ~ *akeru*, *close*/*simaru* ~ *simeru*, *split*/*wareru* ~ *waru*, *bend*/*magaru* ~ *mageru*.

The intransitive/transitive distinction is one aspect of the valency of verbs. The term 'valency' is borrowed from chemistry, where it refers to the combining power of an atom. Applied to verbs, it refers to the number and type of central nouns or other dependent words which a given verb typically combines with in a sentence. Verbs may be thought of as being equipped with associated frames into which nouns are slotted in order to fill out the essential details of the situation they describe. Thus a verb like *kowareru* 'become broken' expects a single noun, marked basically by the case particle *ga*, referring to the thing which becomes broken (*Terebi ga kowareta* 'The television broke down', etc.), while *kowasu* 'break (something)' expects two nouns, marked by *ga* and *o*, referring to the person who does the breaking and the thing which is broken, respectively (*Kodomo ga terebi o kowasita* 'The child broke the television'). Verbs may differ not just in the number of associated nouns but also in their type in terms of the case particles by which they are marked. Thus the verb *iku* 'go' expects two nouns, referring to the person who goes (marked by *ga*) and to the destination (marked by *ni* or *e*): *Kodomo ga gakkoo ni itte iru* (*kara*) '(Since) the child is at (has gone to) school'. A verb such as *kasu* 'lend, rent out' expects three nouns: a lender (*ga*), a thing which is lent (*o*) and a recipient (*ni*). Japanese verbs may have different valencies than their nearest English translation equivalent may suggest; moreover, a single verb may have more than one associated valency frame. Both these possibilities are illustrated by the common verb *au* 'see (and talk with), meet'. This verb has a valency of two, with the principal actor marked by *ga* and the other party marked by *ni* or *to* (not *o*, as English might lead us to expect), according to whether the meeting is presented as one-sided (*ni*) or as a mutual encounter (*to*). In such cases in particular, it is clearly important to learn verbs complete with their associated frames.

Finally, verbs may be volitional or non-volitional. Only volitional verbs occur in the imperative and in the hortative with its basic intentional meaning ('let's ... '). Verbs like *kau* 'buy' and *iru* 'be located (of animates)' are volitional (*Atarasii kuruma o kae* 'Buy a new car!', *Koko ni iyoo* 'Let's stay here'), whereas *tukareru* 'become tired' and *aru* 'be located (of inanimates)' are non-volitional. In addition, volitional verbs combine with a wider range of auxiliary verbs, and there are other grammatical differences. Semantically, volitional verbs typically denote actions controlled by a human actor.

Adverbs

Adverbs are words that—not being members of other word classes—characteristically function to modify verbs, adjectives or other adverbs. As we have seen, in *Kono kuruma wa yoku hasiru* 'This car runs well', *yoku* 'well' is an adverb modifying the verb *hasiru*, and in *sugoku hurui kuruma* 'an amazingly old car', *sugoku* is an adverb modifying the adjective *hurui*. In *Kono kuruma wa sugoku yoku hasiru* 'This car runs amazingly well', the adverb *yoku* is in turn modified by *sugoku*. Some adverbs also form predicates with the copula: in *hazimete au* 'meet for the first time' *hazimete* modifies the verb *au*, but one may also say *Hazimete da* 'It's the first time'. Semantically, many adverbs express manner (like *yoku*) or degree (cf. *motto* 'more', *sukkari* 'completely'), and other common categories include time (like *hazimete*; cf. also *moo* 'already, now', *mada* 'still, (not) yet') and frequency (cf. *tokidoki* 'sometimes', also *yoku* 'often').

As in most languages, many Japanese adverbs are derived from adjectives. In the case of *i* adjectives these end in *-ku* (like *yoku* and *sugoku*); with *na* adjectives they are generally marked by *ni* (*kiree ni* 'beautifully', *zyoozu ni* 'skilfully'), and with *no* adjectives often by *de* (*hadaka de* 'naked(ly)'). Adverbs are occasionally also derived from nouns (like *tokidoki*) or verbs (like *hazimete*). In addition, Japanese has a large number of imitative or mimetic adverbs; these are often marked, optionally or obligatorily, by *to*: cf. *berabera* (*to*) 'volubly', *hakkiri* (*to*) 'clearly', *nikkori* (*to*) 'with a smile', *gurut to* '(go around) in a circle', *pokiN to* '(break) with a snap', etc.

This concludes our survey of the lexical word classes of Japanese. Other, closed classes (such as the copula and various kinds of 'particles') are found within grammar. Also within grammar belong closed subclasses of some of the word types considered here, notably grammatical nouns of various kinds (such as *koto*, *hoo*, etc.) and grammatical verbs (such as *iru*, *oku*, etc. in their use as auxiliaries). These will be considered in chapter 5.

Origins

By any standards, Japanese has borrowed heavily from other languages: in terms of dictionary entries, loanwords account for about 60 per cent of the modern vocabulary. The vast majority of these borrowings are from classical Chinese and from Western languages, most notably English. Large-scale borrowing of this kind arises where donor languages are seen as carriers of a prestigious civilization, and on a historical level the presence of these loans reflects the two major external influences on the course of Japan's development.

They are also of major importance for the structure of the modern Japanese vocabulary. (Grammar is generally much less susceptible to external influence of this kind, and grammatical items are overwhelmingly native.) The two main strands of Japanese borrowings have come from languages to which it is unrelated genetically and typologically and which, moreover, are unrelated to each other. This has contributed to the status of loanwords as relatively clear-cut groups in the vocabulary as a whole.

Sino-Japanese words

Sino-Japanese (SJ) words—i.e. words borrowed from, or coined in Japan on the basis of, classical Chinese—have been estimated to account for more than half of the total Japanese word stock. As discussed in the previous chapter, borrowing from Chinese dates back at least 1500 years and has been accompanied by the adoption and subsequent Japanization of the Chinese character script. As a result the SJ vocabulary is solidly established in the language and, despite its Chinese origin, is not felt as 'foreign' in the same way as are Western loanwords.

Nevertheless SJ items show several characteristic features. Perhaps the most notable is that SJ morphemes (such as *sui* 'water', *tai* 'big', *boku* 'tree, wood') do not generally function as independent words, so that SJ words typically contain two morphemes. Basic vocabulary items such as *niNgeN* 'man, human being', *gakusee* 'student', *doobutu* 'animal', *kaisya* 'company', *deNki* 'electricity', *gakkoo* 'school', *kuukoo* 'airport', *ryoori* 'cuisine', *syuppatu* 'departure', *beNkyoo* 'study', *saNpo* 'walk, stroll', *siNsetu na* 'kind', *geNki na* 'in good spirits' are all SJ 'binary' words of this type. SJ morphemes come in a limited number of shapes, and some of these are subject to automatic changes when combined in binary words. The word *gakkoo* 'school', for example, results from the combination of *gaku* + *koo*, *syuppatu* 'departure' from *syutu* + *hatu*, and *saNpo* 'walk, stroll' from *saN* + *ho*.

In writing, of course, SJ words are normally written in the kanji script. The connection with kanji is often essential, since the relatively small number of SJ morpheme shapes tends to give rise to homophones (i.e. different words which sound alike); even medium-sized dictionaries list more than a dozen words pronounced *koosyoo*, which are only distinguished in writing thanks to the morphemic script. The kanji script often serves also to link the SJ and native vocabulary, in that many kanji, as we have seen, have both on- and kun-readings: SJ *sui* 'water' is linked to native *mizu* '(cold) water' through being written with the same kanji 水.

SJ loanwords occur as nouns, as *na* and *no* adjectives and as adverbs, as well as combining with the native item *suru* 'do' to form hybrid verbs: *syuppatusuru* 'depart', *beNkyoosuru* 'study', *koosyoosuru* 'negotiate', etc. Many SJ words are firmly entrenched in the everyday vocabulary, as illustrated by the examples above. Others are associated with the written language, some very strongly; most 'difficult' words in Japanese, learned via writing, are SJ.

Western loanwords

Western (WJ) loanwords are currently dominated by borrowings from English. This has not always been the case. Japan's earliest Western contacts, dating from the sixteenth century, were chiefly with the Portuguese and the Dutch, and many everyday loanwords survive from this time: e.g. *paN* 'bread', *tabako* 'cigarette', *botaN* 'button' (from Portuguese); *koohii* 'coffee', *biiru* 'beer', *koppu* 'tumbler', *garasu* 'glass (substance)', *peNki* 'paint', *gomu* 'rubber' (from Dutch). In this century, and particularly since World War II, the influence of (British and American) English has been all-pervasive, with loans from German and French also notable in particular fields. Existing surveys of dictionary entries indicate a WJ presence of around 6 per cent, with some 80 per cent of these loans stemming from English.

WJ items stand out most clearly in writing, where they are generally represented in katakana supplemented with various special conventions. These in turn reflect the wider range of sound combinations found in these words, and WJ loans in general make freer use of the resources of the Japanese sound system. They occur chiefly as nouns and *na* adjectives and, like SJ loans, combine with *suru* to form verbs (e.g. *pasusuru* 'pass (an exam)', *saiNsuru* 'sign (a document)', etc.). Interestingly, some also occur as word components rather than as words in their own right; an example is *Tii* (from *tea*), which occurs in words such as *aisuTii*, *Tiibaggu*, etc.

Clearly English loanwords are a welcome presence in the language for English-speaking learners. They are not, however, entirely problem-free. In the first place, we have seen that they must be adapted to the Japanese sound system. While general rules can be given for transferring English sound shapes into Japanese, these do not enable us to predict the actual shape of existing loanwords with certainty. One reason for this is that the rules of transfer have changed over time, and established loanwords may have been borrowed under different rules. An example is provided by the treatment of the sound *k* in loanwords. Nowadays where an additional Japanese vowel needs to be supplied after this sound, *u* is added, as in *burakku* (from *black*), *baiku* (*bike*), *maaku* (*mark*), etc. However, at an earlier stage Japanese *i* was added in such cases, and several common loanwords preserve this correspondence: e.g. *keeki* (from *cake*), *bureeki* (*brake*), *sakisohoN* (*saxophone*). This type of variation is illustrated particularly clearly where the same English word has been borrowed at different periods (with different meanings). For example the English word *strike* has given rise to two Japanese loans, the older *sutoraiki* '(workers') strike' and the more recent *sutoraiku* 'strike (in baseball)'.

Another reason is that the form of the Japanese loan is often influenced by English spelling. In some cases this influence is general, and the correspondences concerned form part of the regular transfer rules. Thus English words spelt with final *-ng* regularly end in *Ngu* (rather than *N*) in Japanese (e.g. *kuriiniNgu* (from *cleaning*), *ibuniNgu* (*evening*), *FookusoNgu* (*folk-song*)—*saaFiN* (*surfing*) is a rare exception here). However, the influence of spelling is often unpredictable, as in loans such as *oobuN* (*oven*), *guroobu* (*glove*), *buzaa* (vs expected *bazaa*: *buzzer*), *airoN* (*iron*), etc, and here too we occasionally find two borrowed forms, one spelling-influenced and one not: besides *airoN* '(clothes) iron' we find the 'expected' *aiaN* 'iron (golf-club)'.

Finally, English loanwords frequently become shortened in Japanese. The following are all everyday examples: *depaato* (*department store*), *terebi* (*television*), *paama* (*permanent wave*), *biru* (*building*), *paNku* (*puncture*), *akuseru* (*accelerator*), *toire* (*toilet*), *eakoN* (*air conditioner*), *nooto* (*notebook*), *ibuniNgu* (*evening dress*). Normally, as here, the tail of the word is discarded, but occasionally the first part of the word is dropped, obscuring the relation with the English source word still further: e.g. *doraibaa* (*screwdriver*), *hoomu* (*platform*), *nekku* (*bottleneck*). All this means that, while we should be aware of general rules of transfer, we must be prepared to find varying degrees of deviation from these in practice.

The meanings of these loanwords also need to be approached with caution. There is a natural tendency for English-speakers to expect their meaning in Japanese to be identical with that of their source words in English, but this is by no means always the case. The meaning of a word depends in part on the meaning of other words which surround it in the vocabulary; in entering Japanese, loanwords take up position among a new set of companions, and this often involves subtle changes in meaning and use. An important principle here is that the loanwords frequently take on a narrower meaning in Japanese, with their semantic range restricted to modern, Western-style situations in contrast to existing Japanese words. The word *raisu* (from *rice*) is an obvious example. In English *rice* is a general term, but in Japanese *raisu* denotes boiled rice served Western-style, in contrast to *gohaN*. Similarly, *biru* (from *building*) denotes a building of a specific type, namely a modern-style office building. Examples can be readily multiplied: *naihu* (from *knife*) is applied to table knives, but not to Japanese kitchen knives, which are *hootyoo*; *resiito* (from *receipt*) refers to the printed slips produced by cash registers, not to written receipts (*ryoosyuusyo*); and *burasi* (from *brush*) denotes brushes used for cleaning rather than brushes used for applying solutions, which are *hake*. Many cases of semantic skewing are more blatant than these (e.g. *haNdoru* (from *handle* (?)) 'steering wheel', *maNsyoN* (*mansion*) '(modern-style) apartment', *sutoobu* (*stove*) 'heater', *manikyua* (*manicure*) 'nail polish'), and in some cases the semantic link may be completely obscure (e.g. *baikiNgu* (*viking*) 'buffet-style cuisine', *hotikisu* (*Hotchkiss*) 'stapler', *gaado* (*girder bridge* (?)) 'railway overpass (near station)').

Finally, most foreign proper names, of both places and persons, are WJ items. Place names are often borrowed from English, but there are many notable exceptions. Names of several European countries, for example, stem from Portuguese or Dutch, including *igirisu* 'Britain', *oraNda* 'Holland', *girisya* 'Greece', *doitu* 'Germany' as does *yooroppa* 'Europe' itself; *itaria* 'Italy', *suisu* 'Switzerland' and *berugii* 'Belgium' also derive from non-English sources. In addition, names of cities are sometimes borrowed from the local language; examples include *pari* 'Paris', *uiiN* 'Vienna', *myuNheN* 'Munich', *puraha* 'Prague', *rooma* 'Rome', *atene* 'Athens', *mosukuwa* 'Moscow', *erusaremu* 'Jerusalem'. Interestingly, familiar Chinese city names follow English (e.g. *pekiN* 'Peking', *syaNhai* 'Shanghai', *hoNkoN* 'Hong Kong'), but are often written in kanji.

Native words

The remaining vocabulary—with the exception of a small number of long-standing and well-integrated loanwords from neighbouring languages, including Ainu—is native in origin. Native vocabulary occurs in all word classes, including in particular the inflected classes of verbs and *i* adjectives. These resist the direct incorporation of loanwords, and virtually all basic verbs (as opposed to verbs formed with *-suru*) and *i* adjectives are native. In writing, native vocabulary is commonly written in kanji (combined with hiragana in inflected words), and almost all kanji are in turn linked with SJ morphemes.

Within the native vocabulary, imitative or mimetic words stand out clearly as a special structural group. Further examples of these words are: *poN to* 'casually', *gyut to* 'tightly', *sassa to* 'hurriedly', *byuubyuu (to)* 'howlingly', *daraN to* 'limply', *basat to* 'with a flap', *yaNwari (to)* 'softly', *tiratira (to)* 'flickeringly'. Mimetics are characterized by their use of a wide range of sounds (for example, initial *p* is common in these words, but is otherwise found only in Western loanwords), and in writing they are represented in hiragana or katakana, not in kanji. They are also formed according to a limited number of patterns, most commonly the addition of *-t* (*gyut to*, *basat to*), of

-*N* (*poN to*, *daraN to*), of *-ri* (*yaNwari (to)*), or reduplication (*sassa to*, *byuubyuu (to)*, *tiratira (to)*). The mimetic bases themselves, to which these processes are applied, consist of one short syllable (e.g. *gyu-*, *po-*, *sa-*) or, much more commonly, two short syllables (e.g. *basa-*, *dara-*, *yawa-*, *tira-*). One base often produces a series of mimetic words, which are normally closely related in meaning: from *poki-*, for example, are formed *pokit to*, *pokiN to*, *pokiri (to)*, *pokkiri (to)* and *pokipoki (to)*, all denoting snapping noises. The main semantic difference among these is that the reduplicated word, *pokipoki (to)*, denotes a series of such noises, whereas the others refer to a single sound. While some items have developed very general meanings (e.g. *tyotto* 'a little', *tyaNto* 'properly', *sukkari* 'completely'), mimetics typically refer to highly specific sounds, sights, movements, textures, sensations and emotions.

Mimetic words occur basically as adverbs, where they are often closely associated with particular verbs: e.g. *pokit to oreru* 'break with a snap', *berabera syaberu* 'talk volubly', *bissyori nureru* 'get soaking wet', etc. Many also forms verbs in combination with *suru*: *bikkurisuru* 'be surprised' and *hirihirisuru* 'smart (of pain)' are dynamic verbs, *assarisite iru* 'be plain, simple' and *deppurisite iru* 'be plump' are stative verbs, occurring as predicates in combination with *iru*. Finally, we have seen that some mimetics also form *no*-adjectives: *bisyobisyo no* 'soaked', *garagara no* 'deserted', etc.

Mimetics are an interesting and important group of words that add colour and vividness to Japanese speech. Special Japanese mimetic dictionaries contain well over a thousand entries, and learners should be familiar with their general structural principles.

Word formation

Unlike grammar, which changes only slowly over time, the vocabularies of languages are continually adding new words (and abandoning old ones) in response to changes in the everyday life of their speakers. One major source of new words is borrowing. In addition, all languages possess ways of building new words out of material already present in their vocabularies. This process of building new words out of old is known as 'word formation', and words formed in this way are 'complex words'.

There are two main methods of building new words. One is to take two existing words and join them together; this is known as 'compounding'. English words such as *paper-clip*, *greenhouse* and *sky-blue* are compounds. The other is to take a single word and effect some kind of change on it; this is 'derivation'. The change may involve adding an affix (as in English *farmer*, derived from *farm*) or changing the word class of the word without further modification (e.g. the English verb *chair (a meeting)*, derived from the noun *chair*), and various other processes are found. While compounding and derivation are universal processes, languages differ in the details of their operation. A large proportion of everyday vocabulary is made up of complex words, and learners need to be aware of the main features of word formation in Japanese.

Compounding

A wide range of compounds are found in Japanese: cf. *huruhoN* 'second-hand book' (*hurui* 'old' + *hoN* 'book'), *kamibukuro* 'paper bag' (*kami* 'paper' + *hukuro* 'bag'), *oyako* 'parent and child' (*oya* 'parent' + *ko* 'child'), *otokokyoodai* 'brothers' (*otoko* 'man' + *kyoodai* 'brothers and sisters'), *hosonagai* 'elongated' (*hosoi* 'thin, slender' + *nagai* 'long'), *yakitori* 'chicken kebab' (*yaku* 'fry, roast' + *tori* 'chicken'), *tumekiri* 'nail clippers' (*tume* 'nail' + *kiru* 'cut'), *gozioki* 'rising at five o'clock' (*gozi* 'five o'clock' + *okiru* 'get up'), *tobioriru* 'jump down' (*tobu* 'jump' + *oriru* 'descend').

These examples illustrate several points. First, compounds belong in various word classes: we have compound nouns (like *huruhoN* and the majority of the examples), but also compound adjectives (like *hosonagai*) and compound verbs (like *tobioriru*).

Secondly, we find various combinations of word classes among the components: *huruhoN* combines an adjective with a noun, *yakitori* a verb with a noun, *tumekiri* a noun with a verb and so on. Note that when verbs and *i* adjectives (i.e. inflected words) enter into word formation, they generally appear in a distinct 'stem' form. In the case of most verbs, this involves replacement of the final -*u* of the non-past by -*i* (cf. *kiru* 'cut': *kiri*-); for some verbs and for *i* adjectives, it is the non-past form minus the -*ru* or -*i* ending (cf. *okiru* 'get up': *oki*-, *hurui* 'old': *huru*-).

Thirdly, we see that compounding may be accompanied by certain sound changes, as in *kamibukuro* (from *kami* + *hukuro*). This particular change is known as rendaku and involves the second component in compounds. Where this component begins with one of the voiceless sounds *k*/*s*/*t*/*h*, these may be replaced by the voiced sounds *g*/*z*/*d*/*b* (cf. also *megusuri* 'eye drops' (*me* 'eye' + *kusuri* 'medicine'), *haizara* 'ashtray' (*hai* 'ash' + *sara* 'plate'), *hoNdana* 'bookshelf' (*hoN* 'book' + *tana* 'shelf')).

Rendaku mainly affects native words and its operation is somewhat unpredictable. One situation in which it never occurs is in co-ordinating compounds such as *oyako* 'parent and child' (not *oyago): the meaning of these compounds is basically 'X and Y', and other examples include *asabaN* 'morning and evening' (*asa* 'morning' + *baN* 'evening, night'), *teasi* 'limbs' (*te* 'hand' + *asi* 'leg, foot'), *noriori* 'getting on and off' (*noru* 'get on' + *oriru* 'descend'). Co-ordinating compounds are not found in all languages. Note that English, for example, generally makes use of phrases with the word *and* in such cases.

It is important to note that, as far as the regular processes of word formation are concerned, Sino-Japanese binary words are treated as simple, indivisible units. Thus, in *otokokyoodai* 'brothers', the SJ word *kyoodai* enters into compounding as a ready-made word; *kyoodai* itself is not an ordinary compound (since *kyoo* and *dai* are not words), and the principles of formation of these SJ binary words lie outside the mainstream processes. *Otokokyoodai* also illustrates the point that Japanese compounds may combine words of different origins (here, native + SJ). Other combinations occur in *haburasi*

'toothbrush' (native: *ha* 'tooth' + WJ: *burasi* 'brush') and
deNkisutoobu 'electric heater' (SJ: *deNki* 'electricity' + WJ:
sutoobu 'heater').

Note also that, once words are borrowed into Japanese,
they are free to form compounds that may have no counterparts in the original language. The most obvious examples are
of so-called 'Japanese–English', where English loanwords are
combined in novel combinations: e.g. *gasoriNsutaNdo* 'petrol
station', *dekoreesyoNkeeki* 'large fancy cake', *goorudeNuiiku*
'week in April–May which contains several national holidays',
etc.

Derivation
Derivation produces a new word by effecting some process of
modification on an existing word. We shall consider three
main types of derivation in Japanese: affixation (the addition
of an affix), conversion (the changing of word-class membership with no addition of material) and reduplication (the
doubling of a word).

Affixation bears some resemblance to compounding in that
it involves the combination of two distinct items. (Moreover,
affixes often develop historically from words.) However, affixes are generally specialized as to position (in Japanese, as prefixes or as suffixes), and they tend to be added only to words
of a particular group (e.g. in terms of word class, meaning or
origin).

Japanese has far more suffixes than prefixes. One of the most
important prefixes is the so-called 'honorific' prefix *o-*, which
is added to nouns (e.g. *onamae* 'name (of respected person)',
okane 'money', *oyasai* 'vegetables'), adjectives (e.g. *oisogasii*
'busy (of respected person)', *ozyoozu na* 'skilful (of respected
person)') and verbs (in the stem form) (e.g. *onomi (ni naru)*
'drink (of respected person)', *okaesi (suru)* 'return (to respected
person)'). While many of the resulting derivatives are indeed
honorific, referring to respected persons, to their actions or
possessions, or to actions affecting them, this is not always the
case. In words such as *okane* or *oyasai*, *o-* functions rather as a

'softening' prefix. Thus *okane* is the most general word for 'money', the unprefixed *kane* being rather a robust term, and *oyasai* 'vegetables' is a specifically feminine term, contrasting with the more general *yasai*. A further prefix, *go-*, is more generally honorific, but combines almost exclusively with SJ words (cf. *gozyuusyo* 'address (of respected person)', *goikeN* 'opinion (of respected person)', etc.).

Among suffixes, several function to change word-class membership rather than to add specific meanings: these 'general' suffixes include *-sa* '-ness' (produces nouns from adjectives: *ookisa* 'size'), *-teki na* '-ic' (adjectives from nouns: *kagakuteki na* 'scientific'), *-ppoi* '-ish' (adjectives from various classes: *mizuppoi* 'watery', *wasureppoi* 'forgetful'), *-suru* (verbs from nouns and mimetic adverbs: *syuppatusuru* 'depart', *hakkirisuru* 'become clear', *bakuzeNtosite iru* 'be vague'), *-garu* 'show signs of' (verbs from subjective adjectives: *itagaru* 'show signs of being in pain').

There is a vast range of more specific suffixes. One interesting group is composed of verbal suffixes that refine the meanings of other verbs in various ways: cf. *-dasu* 'begin suddenly (to do)' (*huridasu* 'begin to fall (of rain, etc.)'), *-au* '... each other' (*tasukeau* 'help each other'), *-naosu* 're-' (*kaNgaenaosu* 'rethink'), *-sugiru* '(do) excessively' (*nomisugiru* 'drink too much'; also added to adjectives: *nagasugiru* 'be too long'). There are many SJ, as well as native, affixes; a rare WJ affix is *-maN* 'man' (cf. *syoosyamaN* 'trading company employee').

Conversion is sometimes described as 'zero derivation'; like much affixation, it derives a new word belonging to a different word class, but no extra material is added in the process. The major case of conversion in Japanese involves the derivation of nouns from verbs (in their stem forms): cf. *hanasi* 'talk, story, matter' (from *hanasu* 'speak'), *kaNgae* 'idea' (*kaNgaeru* 'think'), *hazime* 'beginning' (*hazimeru* 'begin'), *owari* 'end' (*owaru* 'end'), *kaNzi* 'feeling, impression' (*kaNziru* 'feel'). We have also treated the formation of Japanese adverbs from adjectives as conversion (*sugoku* 'amazingly', *zyoozu ni* 'skilfully' from the corresponding forms of *sugoi* 'amazing', *zyoozu na* 'skilful', etc.), and we have seen a further case in the derivation of *no* adjectives from certain mimetic adverbs, as in *pikapika no* 'sparkling (clean)' from *pikapika (to)* 'flashingly'.

Finally, Japanese also derives new words by reduplication. Here the form of a word is doubled, and rendaku commonly occurs. Examples include reduplicated nouns such as *hitobito* 'people' (from *hito* 'person'), *kuniguni* 'countries' (*kuni* 'country'), *yamayama* 'mountains' (*yama* 'mountain')—these have a somewhat literary flavour—but most reduplicated words are adverbs (cf. *naganaga (to)* 'at great length' (from *nagai* 'long'), *hayabaya (to)* 'quickly' (*hayai* 'early, fast'), *ariari to* 'vividly' (*aru* 'be located (of inanimates)', etc.). Reduplication is particularly prevalent in mimetic words, where it is never accompanied by rendaku: *tiratira (to)* 'flickeringly' and not **tirazira (to)*, *hirihiri (to)* 'smartingly' and not **hiribiri (to)*, etc. Semantically, reduplication is commonly associated with plurality, repetition, continuity or intensification.

Clipping

Japanese has other ways of forming new words in addition to the major processes outlined above. The main one of these involves shortening or 'clipping'. Clipping simply discards some portion of a word and generally results in a more colloquial version of the original. Familiar examples from English include *pro* (from *professional*), *ad* (*advertisement*), *phone* (*telephone*), etc.

We have seen that many Western loanwords occur in shortened forms in Japanese. Often the clipped form is the only one in common use, but in some cases both forms occur (e.g. *asuparagasu/asupara* 'asparagus', *ootomatikku/ootoma* 'automatic (transmission)', *purattohoomu/ hoomu* 'platform'). Clipping of this kind also occurs in some composite words, as in *basutee(ryuuzyo)* 'bus stop', *kyuukoo(ressya)* 'express (train)', *teeki(keN)* 'commuter pass', etc. With some compounds, a more complex type of clipping is found, involving cuts in each component of the word. A typical example is the word *tokkyuu* 'special express', formed from *toku(betu)kyuu(koo)*; cf.

also *nyuu(gaku)si(keN)* 'entrance exam', *sotu(gyoo)roN(buN)* 'fourth-year thesis', *too(kyoo)dai(gaku)* 'Tokyo University', *kyoo(to)dai(gaku)* 'Kyoto University', etc. *Koo(toogak)koo* 'upper secondary school, senior high school' shows a slightly different pattern. This type of clipping is mainly associated with Sino-Japanese compounds, but it is sometimes extended beyond these: *waa(do)puro(sessaa)* 'word processor', *razi(o)-kase(tto)* 'cassette radio' and *paN(Tii)suto(kkiNgu)* 'pantyhose' are common Western loanwords treated in the same way.

Idioms: Multi-word units

Although they lie strictly outside the concerns of the present section, this is a convenient place to refer briefly to Japanese idioms. Idioms occur in all languages, and they constitute a second major type of vocabulary unit together with lexical words. Superficially, idioms look like ordinary grammatical combinations of words (i.e. phrases or sentences), but their special status lies precisely in the fact that they are not what they seem: in one way or another—in grammatical behaviour, in meaning, etc.—they are idiosyncratic, and they require dictionary treatment as individual units.

Idioms in this sense take in a wide range of multi-word expressions, including proverbs (e.g. *Saru mo ki kara otiru* 'Monkeys also fall from trees, i.e. Everyone makes mistakes'), fixed similes (e.g. *neko no hitai hodo no* 'about the size of a cat's forehead, i.e. tiny (in area)') and social formulas (e.g. *Akemasite omedetoogozaimasu* 'Happy New Year'), as well as more semantically opaque expressions which are often thought of as idioms par excellence. Many of these latter feature noun + verb or noun + adjective predicative combinations in Japanese: cf. *hara ga tatu* 'guts stand up, i.e. become angry', *uma ga au* 'horses fit, i.e. get along well (with)', *sazi o nageru* 'throw a spoon, i.e. give up (on)', *atama ni kuru* 'come to one's head, i.e. get mad'; *kao ga hiroi* 'face is broad, i.e. well-known, well-connected', *hito ga ii* 'person is good, i.e. good-natured', *kuti ga warui* 'mouth is bad, i.e. sharp-tongued'. A significant number of common idioms of this type include the noun *ki* 'consciousness, feelings, etc.' and refer to psychological events and qualities: cf. *ki ga tuku* '*ki* attaches, i.e. become aware (of)', *ki ga sumu* '*ki* ends, i.e. feel satisfied', *ki o tukeru* 'attach *ki*, i.e. take care, pay attention', *ki ni naru* 'become *ki*, i.e. become a worry', *ki ga hayai* '*ki* is fast, i.e. impetuous', *ki ga tiisai* '*ki* is small, i.e. faint-hearted'.

Meaning

The most obvious feature of words is that they have meanings. Meanings are elusive entities, and in the initial stages of language-learning it is perhaps natural to assume that the meanings of words in different languages, such as Japanese and English, correspond on a one-to-one basis. This assumption implies that the world of human experience is divided up everywhere in the same way and that the vocabularies of different languages simply attach their own labels to these pre-existing categories; learning the meanings of foreign words is thus a matter of learning to replace English terms with their equivalents in the new language.

Needless to say, this is an erroneous view. In the first place, there are cases where the world of our experience is manifestly not the same in different localities: for example, a desert environment differs markedly from that of a tropical rainforest, and differences of this kind will be reflected in the vocabularies of languages from these regions. Secondly, and more generally, even where we are dealing with what is objectively the 'same' reality, languages may differ in the way they divide up this reality in their vocabularies. Thus the structure of the human body is broadly identical across the species, but languages differ widely in the semantic distinctions which they draw in their body-part vocabularies. In this sense, meanings are internal to particular languages.

This does not mean that languages are not inter-translatable. Rather, what one language describes with a single word, another language may describe with a phrase (i.e. a grammatical combination of words) or with different words on different occasions. It certainly does mean that, as learners, we must expect to find that semantic differences between English and Japanese words are the rule rather than the exception. We must understand that one-to-one equivalences (*'mizu = water'*, etc.), though sometimes suggested by glossaries and dictionaries, are rarely satisfactory, and are generally to be regarded as no more than rough indications of the meanings of Japanese words. In addition, we should endeavour to see Japanese words as being located within groups of semantically associated terms. As we have seen in connection with English loanwords, the meaning of a word is influenced by other words which surround it in the vocabulary; knowing which words contrast semantically with a given term, and which words commonly accompany it in sentences, is an important aspect of fully understanding its meaning.

English/Japanese contrasts

Semantic skewing between basic English and Japanese words can be illustrated from virtually any field in the vocabulary. A commonplace example is:

water	*mizu* '(cold) water'
	oyu '(hot) water'

Here the range of a single word in English is covered by two distinct words in Japanese: in Japanese, *oyu*, not *mizu*, is used for making tea, and it is normally *oyu*, not *mizu*, which one finds in the bathtub (unless it has gone cold, i.e. *mizu ni nattyatta* 'has become *mizu*'). English-speaking learners are prone to errors in cases of this kind, since they need to acquire a lexical distinction not made in their own language. A further basic example involves verbs of giving:

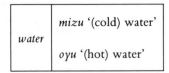

give	*kureru* '*give* (to me, us, etc.)'
	ageru '(I/we, etc.) give'

The distinction between the Japanese verbs here is based on the direction of the giving, viewed from the standpoint of the speaker, and may be compared to the difference between *come* and *go*: *kureru* denotes 'incoming' giving, *ageru* 'outgoing' giving. Japanese in fact has several other verbs of giving that relate to this basic pair, and they are also important in grammar, where they occur as auxiliary verbs.

While cases of this kind are commonplace, the opposite situation also occurs:

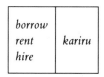

Here Japanese has one word where English has several, and the Japanese-speaking learner of English must learn to distinguish lexically between *borrow* (i.e. for free) and *rent* or *hire* (i.e. for payment). It is also important for English-speakers to be aware of the wider range of *kariru*, which means something like 'obtain temporary use of (whether in return for payment or not)' and should not be glossed simply as 'borrow'.

Mismatches are frequently more complicated than either of these examples. It may be that each language has a series of words, with divisions drawn throughout in different places, as with cooking verbs:

toast	
grill	
barbecue	yaku
bake	
roast	
fry	
	itameru
	ageru

It is clearly important here to understand the basic meaning of *yaku*, which is something like 'cook by the direct application of heat (with or without a small amount of oil)'. *Itameru* is 'stir-fry' and *ageru* 'deep-fry'; however, these processes are both commonly referred to as 'frying' in everyday English, whereas *itameru* and *ageru* are basic terms in Japanese. Once again, it seems desirable that the basic set of cooking terms should be introduced together, with a broad indication of their overall semantic organization.

These examples clearly illustrate the language-internal nature of meanings, and they can be readily multiplied. In some cases, lexical differences can be plausibly related to differences in culture. Given the important place of rice in Japanese life, for example, it is not surprising that Japanese makes a greater number of lexical distinctions than English in this area. Lexical distinctions reflecting traditional vs modern cultural spheres, discussed in connection with Western loanwords, are further examples. In a sense the most extreme cases of this kind occur with objects and institutions which are completely absent from the other culture. Words denoting traditional Japanese furnishings (*tatami* 'floor matting', *syoozi* 'sliding door with translucent paper'), clothing (*yukata* 'cotton kimono', *tabi* 'Japanese-style socks'), foods (*kamaboko* 'fish-paste sausage', *nattoo* 'fermented soya beans'), etc. are examples of basic Japanese terms which can at best be roughly paraphrased in English and which require more direct methods of illustration for full understanding.

This is also the place to elaborate on our earlier discussion of honorifics in Japanese, since they regularly give rise to additional lexical distinctions vis-à-vis English and clearly reflect greater cultural concern with the expression of deference. Honorifics (more precisely, 'referent honorifics') encode respect on the part of the speaker to the person talked about (the 'respected person (RP)') and contrast with non-honorific ('neutral') terms which encode no such respect. All languages permit the signalling of respect—in English, the shop assistant's *This gentleman would like a milkshake* is more respectful than *This man would like a milkshake*—but in Japanese (and some other languages) its expression is more pervasive and more highly systematized. Since honorifics express respect to particular persons, they are found among items that refer to the persons themselves (*ano kata* 'that (respected) person' vs neutral *ano hito*), to persons or things associated with them (*gokazoku* 'family (of RP)' vs *kazoku*, *okao* 'face (of RP)' vs *kao*, *odeNwa* 'telephone call (from or to RP)' vs *deNwa*), to their qualities, states and actions (*ogeNki na* 'in good spirits (of RP)' vs *geNki na*, *okaki ni naru* '(RP) writes' vs *kaku*, *kudasaru* '(RP) gives (me, us, etc.)' vs *kureru*) and to actions performed by others which impinge on them (*otodokesuru* 'deliver (to/for RP)' vs *todokeru*, *sasiageru* '(I, we, etc.) give (to RP)' vs *ageru*).

Honorifics are thus found in various word classes, but they are particularly well developed in verbs, where two types need to be distinguished. The first type (commonly termed 'subject-honorifics', also 'exalting verbs') refer to actions performed by the RP. Most Japanese verbs have corresponding subject-honorifics and, as illustrated earlier, the basic pattern for their formation is *o* + verb stem + *ni naru*: thus, *oyomi ni naru* '(RP) reads' vs *yomu*, *oori ni naru* '(RP) descends' vs *oriru*, etc. However, several common verbs have special subject-honorific counterparts that replace (or, occasionally, alternate with) the expected formations. The main examples are shown in table 4.1. The second type (commonly termed 'object-honorifics' or, sometimes, 'humble verbs') refer to actions performed by other persons that impinge on the RP. These are less numerous than subject-honorifics, since they are only available with verbs which refer to actions that directly affect or involve the RP or persons/things associated with them. They are most common with actions that involve the RP as a recipient, beneficiary or source (i.e. 'do to/for/from RP'), and their basic formation pattern is *o* + verb stem + *suru*: thus, *osirasesuru* 'inform (RP)' vs *siraseru*, *omotisuru* 'hold, carry (for RP)' vs *motu*, *okarisuru* 'borrow (from RP)' vs *kariru*, etc. Once again, however, certain common verbs have special object-honorifics as shown in table 4.2.

Table 4.1 Verbs with special subject-honorifics

Neutral verb	Subject-honorific verb
iru 'be located (of animates)' ⎫ *iku* 'go' ⎬ *irassyaru* *kuru* 'come' ⎭	
suru 'do'	*nasaru*
yuu 'say'	*ossyaru*
kureru 'give (me, us, etc.)'	*kudasaru*
taberu 'eat'	*mesiagaru*
nomu 'drink'	*mesiagaru/onomi ni naru*
miru 'see, look at'	*goraN ni naru*
sitte iru 'know'	*gozoNzi da*

Table 4.2 Verbs with special object-honorifics

Neutral verb	Object-honorific verb
yuu 'say'	*moosiageru*
ageru '(I, we, etc.) give'	*sasiageru*
morau 'receive'	*itadaku*
miru 'see, look at'	*haikeNsuru*
sitte iru 'know'	*zoNziagete iru*
au 'see (and talk to), meet'	*ome ni kakaru*
kiku 'hear, ask'	*ukagau/okikisuru* ('ask')
tazuneru 'visit'	*ukagau*

The effect of the presence of honorifics in Japanese is thus to produce regular two- or three-way lexical contrasts, differing in social meaning, vis-à-vis English: *read* is *yomu* (neutral) or *oyomi ni naru* (subject-honorific), *say* is *yuu* (neutral), *ossyaru* (subject-honorific) or *moosiageru* (object-honorific), etc. Their use is a pervasive feature of the spoken language and clearly requires a detailed appreciation of the Japanese social order: which categories of persons are appropriately treated as RPs, and are such persons referred to with honorifics in all circumstances? Broadly speaking, RPs are non-familiars who are either one's seniors within the group or else members of other groups, and honorifics are used in the presence of RPs or their associates. Very frequently, the RP is the addressee (i.e. *ossyaru* is frequently to be interpreted as 'you say'), with object-honorifics being used of the speaker's actions affecting him or her (i.e. *moosiageru* is often 'I say (to you)').

Much more could be said about semantic contrasts in the vocabulary. Suffice it to say that they are commonplace and that they are a frequent source of learners' errors, both in production and comprehension, even at highly advanced levels. It is, after all, an entirely natural strategy in language learning to extend the semantic structures of our native languages, and this tendency is encouraged by overly simple presentations of the meanings of Japanese words.

Semantic groups

One way to 'get at' the meanings of Japanese words is through comparing and contrasting them with the meanings of English words, as illustrated above. Another is to give attention to semantic relations that hold among Japanese words themselves.

Words are semantically associated with other words of the same language in a variety of ways, and in general it is helpful to learn them as part of semantic networks rather than as isolated items. An important type of grouping is a 'contrast set', i.e. a set of two or more terms that contrast with each other and thus delimit each other in meaning. *Mizu* and *oyu*, and *kureru* and *ageru*, contrast with each other in this way, as do basic cooking verbs, and we have already suggested that terms of this kind should be learned together. Opposites of various kinds constitute a special kind of contrast set; they are commonly associated with adjectives but are also found among basic nouns (*ue* 'top, place above'/*sita* 'bottom, place below', *mae* 'front, place in front'/*usiro* 'back, place behind', *omote* 'front (surface)'/*ura* 'back (surface)', etc.) and verbs (*noru* 'get on, in'/*oriru* 'get off, out', *kau* 'buy'/*uru* 'sell', *katu* 'win'/*makeru* 'lose', etc.). Some verbal opposites, such as *nureru* 'become wet'/*kawaku* 'become dry', *yaseru* 'become thinner'/*hutoru* 'become fatter', *komu* 'become crowded'/*suku* 'become uncrowded' and *kumoru* 'become cloudy'/*hareru* 'become clear', occur where we find adjectives (*wet*/*dry*, etc.) in English. As the glosses indicate, these are change-of-state verbs in Japanese, and the associated state itself is expressed by combinations with *iru*: *nurete iru* 'be wet'/*kawaite iru* 'be dry', etc. Occasionally, opposites are drawn from different word classes, as with the (irregular) adjective *onazi* 'same' and the verb *tigau* 'be different': *onazi kuruma* 'the same car' vs *tigau kuruma* 'a different car'.

Semantic relations of a different type are those that hold among words which tend to occur together in sentences. Some words are extremely free in this respect; an adjective like *onazi* 'same', for example, can modify virtually any noun, and there is little to say about it on this score. Other items, however, are more restricted and tend to combine with particular words in grammatical constructions.

One important type of association is between verbs and nouns with which they typically co-occur. The verb *huru* 'fall', for example, commonly expects the nouns *ame* 'rain' or *yuki* 'snow', and it is helpful to learn the verb embedded in the resulting common phrases *ame ga huru* 'rain falls, it rains', *yuki ga huru* 'snow falls, it snows'. While the verb *kariru* 'borrow, rent, hire' allows a wide range of nouns denoting borrowed/ rented articles, *ie o kariru* 'rent a house' is a common combination that reinforces the wider meaning of the verb vis-à-vis English *borrow*, as does a phrase such as *itiniti saNzeNeN de kariru* 'rent/hire for 3000 yen a day'. This type of relation can also be approached from the standpoint of nouns, which in some cases expect particular verbs. Thus *ame* 'rain' typically occurs in the actor slot with verbs such as *huru* 'fall', *yamu* 'stop' *(ame ga yamu)* or *agaru* 'clear' *(ame ga agaru)*. To take a wider case, common verbal collocations with the noun *kuruma* 'car' would include *kuruma ni noru* 'get/ride in a car', *kuruma de iku* 'go by car', *kuruma o kau* 'buy a car', *kuruma de okuru* 'take (someone home, etc.) by car', *kuruma o tomeru* 'stop, park a car'. Unremarkable as they may seem, such combinations are part of the basic currency of everyday language, and learning vocabulary in phrases of this kind serves to consolidate grammatical patterns as well as to build up lexical ties.

The other main type of association of this kind is between modifiers and the words they modify ('heads'); as we have seen, nouns are typically modified by adjectives, and verbs and adjectives by adverbs, and various lexical associations are found here. To begin with a wider example, the adjective pairs *hosoi/hutoi* and *usui/atui* are often both translatable by English *thin/thick*. However, *hosoi/hutoi* refer to the diameter of elongated objects, *usui/atui* to the thickness of flat objects. Typical collocations are thus *hosoi ito/asi/kubi* 'thin thread/legs/neck' but *usui hoN/kami/kabe* 'thin book/paper/wall'. Tighter associations are well illustrated by mimetic adverbs, which, as we have seen, are often tied to one or two specific verbs. As further examples, *guruguru (to)* 'round and round' typically co-occurs with *mawaru* 'go around', *tekuteku (to)* with *aruku* 'walk' (*tekuteku aruku* 'foot it') and *gussuri (to)* 'soundly' with the verbs *nemuru* 'sleep' or *neru* 'lie down, go to sleep'. Knowledge of co-occurrences in such cases is clearly quite basic to the correct use and understanding of the word.

Style

As well as having meanings, words have stylistic properties, in terms of the type of circumstances in which they are appropriately used. While many words are neutral in this respect, others are restricted in various ways, for example by being used in writing rather than in speech, by men rather than women, in formal rather than informal situations and so on. The style of a word in this sense may be thought of as what we need to know about it, in addition to its grammatical properties and its meaning, in order to use it correctly. Words that have the same meaning tend to differ in style, since languages do not generally tolerate absolute equivalence between different items. Thus the adjectives *oisii* and *umai* have the same meaning (both 'good(-tasting)'), but *umai* is generally used by male speakers, in relatively informal situations.

Stylistic distinctions are prominent in both the vocabulary and grammar of Japanese, and this is an extremely important area for learners. Style in language is a kind of social convention, in the sense that some items are associated with particular circumstances of language use just as certain styles of dress are seen as appropriate to particular occasions. Using words from the wrong style, or mixing words from different styles, is to use language in a socially incongruous way, and stylistic inappropriateness is responsible for much of the unnatural quality of learners' production in any language. Awareness of stylistic factors is also important for comprehension, in enabling us to draw the correct situational inferences from the utterances we hear or read.

Colloquial and bookish words

We begin with a broad distinction between spoken and written language words. We have seen earlier that spoken and written Japanese are to some extent distinct varieties (or 'mediums'), designed, like spoken and written language everywhere, to fulfil different communicative tasks. While much vocabulary is common to both mediums, some words are more at home in the spoken language—we shall label these 'colloquial'—and other ('bookish') words are associated with the written language.

Much of the character of colloquial vocabulary stems from the more immediate and personal nature of spoken-language communication. Compared with the more weighty, impersonal functions of the written language, conversation in particular gives freer rein to the communication of emotions and attitudes and, naturally enough, it also makes full use of the expressive resources of the sound-system of the language. Thus, among the commonest words in spoken Japanese are the expressive adjectives *sugoi* 'amazing, awful' and *monosugoi* 'terrific, terrible', together with their associated (degree) adverbs *sugoku* and *monosugoku*: *sugoku muzukasii* 'awfully difficult', *monosugoku takai* 'terribly expensive'. Degree adverbs in general readily attract an emotive charge, and items such as *zuibuN*, *totemo*, *iya ni*, *baka ni*, *yake ni*, *metyakutya ni* (all roughly 'very, extremely') are all colloquial. Some items of this kind are further intensified by the doubling of consonants: *tottemo*, for example, is a well-established variant of *totemo*, and *aNmari* '(not) very' generally replaces *amari* in conversation. Some items from other areas of the vocabulary have similar lively colloquial partners (cf. *oNnazi* 'same' vs *onazi*, *iroNna* 'various' vs *iroiro na*), and suffixes incorporating geminates, such as *-kko/-ppo-/-ppa/-kka*, are found in colloquial variants, chiefly of nouns: cf. *hazikko* 'edge' (vs *hazi*), *karappo no* 'empty' (vs *kara no*), *happa* 'leaf' (vs *ha*), *wakka* 'ring, circle' (vs *wa*). These are particularly characteristic of Tokyo Japanese, as are colloquial verbs such as *okkotiru* 'fall'/*okkotosu* 'drop' (vs *otiru*/*otosu*) and *nokkaru* 'get on, in'/*nokkeru* 'place on' (vs *noru*/*noseru*).

Spoken language being typically concerned with the mundane, colloquial terms are prominent in everyday fields of meaning, and some very general words have more colloquial partners in certain uses: cf. *yaru* 'do' vs *suru* (as in *goruhu o yaru* 'play golf'), *yatu* 'thing, one' vs *mono*/*no* (*itigo ga haitte iru yatu* 'the one with the strawberries in'), *toko* 'place' vs *tokoro* (*Ii toko da yo* 'It's a good place'), etc. Spoken language items also vary in type and degree. One group of terms is found in baby-talk, i.e. language addressed to, or used by, small children, and a few terms originating from this source, such as *tittyai* 'weeny' (cf. *tiisai*), *oNbusuru* 'carry on one's back' (cf. *obuu*), *osikko-(suru)* '(do) wee', are used more generally in the spoken language. Other terms are associated with informal male speech and are potentially offensive if used inappropriately; these are considered in the next section.

Whereas colloquial words are predominantly native, written Japanese—which has a much larger vocabulary—is generally characterized by a higher proportion of Sino-Japanese items, and there are many examples where an SJ word is more bookish than a native item of similar meaning. Thus, stylistically neutral native verbs frequently have bookish hybrid counterparts combining SJ items with *suru*: cf. *tukau*/*siyoosuru* 'use', *umu*/*syussaNsuru* 'give birth to', *sinu*/*siboosuru* 'die', *hueru*/*zookasuru* 'increase', *heru*/*geNsyoosuru* 'decrease', etc. There are, however, exceptions to this trend, and neutral/bookish pairs such as *tukau*/*motiiru* 'use' and *tigau*/*kotonaru* 'be different' feature two native verbs. Similarly, by no means all SJ items are bookish, and we also find comparable pairs where both terms are Sino-Japanese: cf. *kazi*/*kasai* 'fire (conflagration)', *kyoosi*/*kyooyu* 'teacher', etc. Finally, it should be stressed that written language, too, takes in a wide variety of subtypes, or genres, and bookish vocabulary varies in character accordingly. There is, for example, a sizeable literary vocabulary associated with traditional Japanese poetry (including such terms as *akebono* 'dawn', *isago* 'sand', *utage* 'banquet'), which is entirely native.

Masculine and feminine words

We have already mentioned several cases of vocabulary items that are associated with male or female users. As in grammar, gender-based vocabulary differences are primarily apparent in the spoken language, so that the items concerned are in general also colloquial. It is helpful to think more generally here, in terms of a stylistic cline ranging from 'genteel' to 'robust'. In Japanese as commonly elsewhere, women typically operate nearer the genteel end of the cline, whereas men's usage ranges more widely and, particularly in informal speech, may take in robust, even 'vulgar', items normally avoided by women. In between is an area where terms are used equally by women and men in less informal circumstances. Needless to say, these distinctions apply only in some areas of the vocabulary; vast numbers of lexical items are completely neutral with respect to this dimension.

A sizeable number of Japanese words are associated with male informal speech; while perfectly appropriate in its place (e.g. in conversation among familiars), some of this vocabulary has a direct quality which may render it offensive in other circumstances. Among nouns of self-reference, *ore* 'I' is a 'macho' term of this type. Also masculine are kinship terms such as *oyazi/oyazisaN* 'father', *ohukuro/ohukurosaN* 'mother', *nyooboo* 'wife' and terms relating to food and eating such as *kuu* 'eat', *mesi* 'boiled rice, meal', *hara ga heru* 'feel hungry' and *umai* 'good(-tasting)'. As indicated earlier, items such as *kane* 'money' are marked as masculine vis-à-vis the prefixed form *okane*. Except for older speakers, the verb *yaru* '(I, we, etc.) give' is nowadays largely restricted to male speech vis-à-vis *ageru*. Beyond commonplace items of this kind we find various deprecatory items that are perhaps characteristic of particular social groups, being encountered in everyday life mainly in gangster movies, comics and the like. They include the interesting category of dishonorifics, i.e. items which encode disrespect to the participants involved: dishonorific verbs are derived with the suffix *-yagaru* (*iku* 'go' → *ikiyagaru* '(the bastard) goes', etc.).

Japanese female speech is marked, in the first place, by the avoidance of masculine terms. Specifically feminine vocabulary items generally involve prefixation with *o-* and are otherwise restricted in number. The expressive adjective *suteki na* 'lovely, super' is definitely feminine in tone, although male speakers sometimes use it empathetically when addressing females, and the degree adverb *totemo/tottemo* 'very' appears also to be used predominantly by females. Feminine items with *o-* prefixation are chiefly nouns from everyday domestic areas of meaning and are illustrated by such examples as *oryoori* 'cooking', *okaimono* 'shopping', *osoozi* 'cleaning'; *osakana* 'fish', *oyasai* 'vegetables', *osio* 'salt', *onabe* 'pan'; *osaihu* 'purse', *onedaN* 'price'; *onikai* 'upstairs', *otoire* 'toilet', etc.

Informal and formal words

'Informal' and 'formal' are broad terms—written-language words, for example, may be said to be more formal than spoken-language items—but our focus here is once more on the spoken language, where we interpret them in terms of the degree of familiarity between speaker and addressee. The notion is thus of a scale of social distance, ranging from informal to formal, and alternative labels might include 'familiar/casual' vs 'distant/stiff'. Formality in this sense is of major importance in Japanese grammar, where it is encoded in inflections, but it is also relevant to the vocabulary.

As indicated above, many masculine items are suitable only for use among familiars and thus qualify as informal. This can be confirmed on the basis of compatibility with inflected forms: the macho item *ore* 'I', for example, combines only with informal forms (*Ore da* 'It's me', but not **Ore desu* (formal) or **Ore degozaimasu* (extra-formal)), whereas *boku* (also 'I', masculine) is freer in this respect (*Boku da/Boku desu/*Boku degozaimasu*), as is the adjective *umai* 'good(-tasting)'. At the opposite end of the scale we find a small set of extra-formal verbs correlating with certain common basic verbs:

Basic verb	Extra-formal verb
aru 'be located (of inanimates)'	*gozaimasu*
iru 'be located (of animates)'	*orimasu*
iku 'go' *kuru* 'come'	*mairimasu*
suru 'do'	*itasimasu*
yuu 'say, be called'	*moosimasu*
siru 'get to know' *omou* 'think'	*zoNzimasu*

These verbs are used in formal circumstances (nowadays, most typically in formal speeches and announcements) where honorifics are also being employed. Confusingly, they have sometimes been labelled 'humble' and grouped together with object-honorifics, but they are to be distinguished from these in that they do not necessarily refer to a human activity impinging on a respected person. For example, one can comment on the arrival of a train with *Mairimasita* '(It) has come'. Outside such cases, they are commonly used to refer to actions of the speaker, but actions of an RP will of course be described by subject-honorifics. It is not clear that other specifically extra-formal vocabulary items exist, but some words combine more readily with these verbs than do others. Thus, both *sakki* and *sakihodo* mean 'just now, a short while ago', but the latter sits more comfortably in the phrase *sakihodo moosimasita yoo ni* 'as I said just now' (with a form of extra-formal *moosimasu*) and is thereby shown to be the more formal word.

Names

Names form an integral part of the vocabulary of a language. We have discussed the treatment of foreign names in Japanese, and in this section we consider briefly some features of Japanese names.

A major general problem of Japanese names, already alluded to, relates to the writing system. In the first place we find an extended range of kanji used in names (including an official list of 284 supplementary kanji approved for use in personal given names). Secondly, many kanji have special readings in names (readings such as *moto*, *yone* and *yosi* for 本、米 and 吉 occur mainly or uniquely in names), and phonetic uses of kanji are also found (as in common names such as *abe* 安部, *kubo* 久保, etc.). There is also a great deal of homophony and homography in Japanese names. Homophonous names sound alike but are written differently; as an example, in a (male) personal name such as *nakagawa kazuo*, *naka* may be written as 中 or 仲, *kawa* as 川 or 河, *kazu* commonly as 一 or 和, and *o* commonly as 夫, 雄 or 男. Homographic names are written alike but are pronounced differently. In the personal name 中田信一, the first two kanji may be read as *nakada* or *nakata* (i.e. with or without rendaku), and possible readings for the second two include *siNiti* and *nobukazu*.

Japanese personal names consist of a family name (*myoozi*) and a single given name (*namae*), in that order. (The word *namae* also has the more general sense of 'personal name'.) Family names are written with one to three kanji, with two-kanji names being overwhelmingly predominant, as in the three most common Japanese family names, *suzuki* (鈴木), *satoo* (佐藤) and *tanaka* (田中). Common three-kanji family names include *sasaki* (佐々木) and *hasegawa* (長谷川), and one-kanji family names *hayasi* (林) and *mori* (森). Family names are read in kun-readings (*suzuki*), on-readings (*satoo*) or in a combination of both (as in *hukuda* 福田). Given names are similar in structure, except that female names are sometimes written wholly or partly in hiragana or katakana. Female given names are particularly associated with the ending *-ko* (子), and many male given names end in *-o* (commonly 男, 夫, 雄), but in Japan as elsewhere given names are subject to fashion and the present trend appears to be away from these patterns.

Place names often also occur as family names, and two-component names again predominate, the most common components including *yama* (山) 'mountain', *kawa* (川, 河) 'river', *ta* (田) 'rice field', *no* (野) 'plain' and *sima* (島) 'island'. Prefecture names are suffixed with *-keN* (県) 'prefecture', with the exception of Osaka and Kyoto prefectures, which attach *-hu* (府) 'urban prefecture' (*oosakahu*, *kyootohu*), and Tokyo, which is in a class of its own and adds *-to* (都) 'metropolis' (*tookyooto*). Most region names, including major islands, are binary SJ words, as *toohoku* (northern Honshu), *kaNtoo* (Tokyo and surrounding prefectures), *kaNsai* (Osaka/Kyoto/Kobe region), *sikoku*, *kyuusyuu*. Other common types of place names include the names of mountains (*huzisaN* 'Mt Fuji'), islands (*awazisima* 'Awaji Island'), rivers (*kamogawa* 'Kamo River'), seas (*nihoNkai* 'Japan Sea'), shrines and temples (*meeziziNguu* 'Meiji Shrine', *eeheezi* 'Eiheiji Temple'), railway lines (*yamano-teseN* 'Yamanote Line'), roads (*toomeekoosoku* 'Tokyo–Nagoya Expressway'), and old province names (*siNsyuu* 'Shinshu'), etc.

While less obvious than personal and place names, various other types of names, both contemporary and historical, are part of the linguistic knowledge of native speakers. Of everyday importance are era names, which are still widely used in dates. These are assigned to the reigns of emperors, of which there have been four during the last century: *meezi* (1868–1912), *taisyoo* (1912–26), *syoowa* (1926–89) and *heesee* (since 1989). Thus 1980 was the fifty-fifth year of Showa (*syoowa gozyuugoneN*) and 1990 the second year of Heisei (*heesee nineN*).

Dictionaries

Kanji dictionaries, both monolingual and bilingual, were discussed in chapter 3; here we consider some of the features of ordinary dictionaries (i.e. 'word dictionaries') of Japanese.

Monolingual dictionaries of Japanese are known as koku-gojiten ('Japanese language dictionaries') and arrange words in the gojuuon order according to their kana spelling. Inflected words (verbs and *i* adjectives) are listed in their non-past form ('dictionary form': かう ('buy'), ふるい ('old'), etc.). Entries typically contain information on kanji spelling (with an indication of its status as officially recommended or otherwise), word class, inflectional class and transitivity (for verbs) and of course meaning; in addition, source language forms are generally given for Western loanwords. Only some dictionaries indicate accentuation, either generally or selectively (e.g. for homophones). One-volume kokugojiten come in two main sizes: concise dictionaries (more compact than their English counterparts) contain in the order of 50 000–70 000 entries, and larger dictionaries (generally called kokugodai-jiten) between two and three times that number.

In any language, ordinary monolingual dictionaries are generally beyond the reach of non-advanced foreign learners, and in Japanese the usual difficulties are compounded by the nature of the writing system. Being designed for native-speaker users, dictionaries of this kind may not include information that is important for the English-speaking learner. As an example, definitions of the verb *kariru* ('borrow, rent, etc.') in these dictionaries make no reference to the fact that it describes both free and paid transactions—just as definitions of *water* in English monolingual dictionaries make no reference to the fact that the substance may be hot or cold. Yet, as we have seen, this is precisely the kind of semantic information that is relevant from a contrastive standpoint, since it reflects differences in Japanese and English lexical structure.

Learners thus naturally turn to bilingual dictionaries, either Japanese–English (waeijiten) or English–Japanese (eiwajiten). However, the vast majority of bilingual dictionaries currently available are designed for Japanese learners of English. In such works illustrative phrases and sentences, as well as explanatory material of various kinds, are written in the regular Japanese script; in English–Japanese dictionaries, this also applies to the

Japanese equivalents themselves. Even where they can be read, these dictionaries are once again not designed to provide all the information on the meaning and use of Japanese words that the English-speaking learner is likely to need.

Specialist dictionaries that are available, dealing with particular aspects of Japanese, are virtually all monolingual and thus of potential interest mainly to advanced learners. Accent dictionaries (akusentojiten) indicate word accentuation and, commonly, some other aspects of word pronunciation; their existence perhaps reflects the absence of accentual information in many general dictionaries. Spelling dictionaries (yoojiyoo-gojiten) deal with various complexities of the orthography and serve as general guides to official recommendations in this area. Loanword dictionaries (gairaigojiten) list Western loan-words, with meanings and foreign-language source words, often with an indication of when the loan entered Japanese; these dictionaries fulfil a clear need to keep pace with the ever-increasing flow of recent borrowings, particularly from English. Mimetic words are not comprehensively listed in general dictionaries, and there are several specialist dictionaries of mimetics (giongitaigojiten), of which some are bilingual (Japanese–English) but require control of the writing system. Finally, dictionaries of synonyms (ruigojiten, ruigigojiten) deal with semantic and stylistic differences between words of similar meaning.

CHAPTER 5

GRAMMAR

Vocabulary provides us with words to describe people, things, qualities, actions and events. In order to communicate with words, we must use them in sentences, and this is the province of grammar.

Grammar has several different aspects. In the first place, for languages which—like English and Japanese—have inflected words, it is concerned with the forms and meanings of the different inflections in which the words occur. Secondly, it is concerned with the use of grammatical words. These are closed sets of words that play important roles in the construction of sentences, for example in linking words and in indicating the relationships between them, or that otherwise express basic communicative notions in the language concerned. Thirdly, when words are combined in sentences they must be arranged in some particular order, and the patterns of ordering found, together with their meanings, are a central concern of grammar.

Languages differ both in the details of these aspects of grammar and in the relative weight they assign to them. Some languages, for example, have no inflected words, and among those that do, inflection varies both in its extent and its complexity. In Japanese, inflection is found in verbs, *i* adjectives and the copula; it is formally relatively straightforward and, importantly for learners, there are few exceptions to the regular patterns. All languages have grammatical words, but their make-up varies considerably. In English, as in many other languages, personal pronouns (*I*, *you*, etc.) form an important class of grammatical words, but we have seen that the separate status of items like *watasi* 'I' in Japanese is much less clear. Finally, languages exhibit different patterns of word order and vary in the rigidity of these patterns. The strongest ordering principle in Japanese is that the predicate (most typically a verb) comes at the end of the sentence; this differs from English, where the verb typically occurs as the second main element, but we have seen that SOV is a common word-order pattern across the languages of the world.

Mastery of the grammar of a foreign language obviously involves acquiring formal control, through memorization and practice, of grammatical forms and patterns. In addition, grammar carries meaning and, as in the vocabulary, languages differ in the semantic distinctions which they choose to express through their grammar. While there is certainly a good deal of overlap between the basic notions encoded in the grammars of English and Japanese, one-to-one correspondence between particular grammatical items in the two languages is rare. To illustrate, the Japanese auxiliary verb *oku* is commonly used together with main verbs to express the meaning '(do) with a view to a future situation': compared with *HoN o kaoo* 'Let's buy a book' without *oku*, *HoN o katte okoo* will be interpreted as 'Let's buy a book e.g. so that we shall have something to read, so that we can refer to it later, so that it will remind us of the occasion, etc.'. English has no single item to convey this meaning, which must be explicitly spelt out through phrases or simply left to be inferred from the context.

A major feature of Japanese grammar is the extent of its incorporation of stylistic information, reflecting the circumstances in which sentences are used. Given the form of a particular Japanese sentence, it is generally possible to tell not only whether it was spoken or written but also, if spoken, whether it was uttered in informal or formal circumstances and, often, whether it was uttered by a male or female speaker. As we have seen, this may be revealed partly by the choice of vocabulary, but it is reflected systematically in grammar—in inflections, in the selection of certain grammatical words and, to some degree, in word order. Clearly, the details of the circumstantial factors involved (e.g. the precise nature of 'informal' and 'formal' situations) once again relate directly to Japanese society.

These factors also complicate the presentation of Japanese grammar. A full treatment must cover all styles, but in an outline description it is more convenient to abstract away from at least some of these distinctions. Our presentation in this chapter will be mainly at the level of the informal spoken language. This is the style first acquired by native speakers and the style generally used within the family and among close friends; moreover, pedagogically the transition from informal to more formal styles is simpler than the reverse. We will, however, omit details of certain contractions and other modifications commonly found in informal speech until the final chapter, where we will also consider other styles. To that extent, our treatment here represents a somewhat idealized version of informal spoken Japanese.

Inflection

Inflection is concerned with the shapes and meanings of different grammatical forms of the same word. In English inflection is found mainly in verbs (*talk, talks, talked, talking, talked*) and nouns (*book, books*), as well as in some adjectives and adverbs (*fast, faster, fastest*). Often we find several formal patterns of inflection within the same word class. For example, in addition to the pattern of *talk*, we find English verb patterns such as *sing, sings, sang, singing, sung* and so on, so that the verbs *talk* and *sing* belong to different inflectional classes. Japanese inflection involves verbs, *i* adjectives and the copula; we shall see that Japanese has few inflectional classes and only a handful of irregular items.

Verbs

We have seen that the non-past form of Japanese verbs ends in *-au, -ou, -uu, -ku, -gu, -su, -tu, -nu, -bu, -mu* or *-ru*. There are two main inflectional classes for verbs ('class 1' and 'class 2'): the rule for membership is that a verb *may* belong to class 2 if and only if its non-past form ends in *-iru* or *-eru*, otherwise it belong to class 1. This is important to understand. An *-iru/-eru* ending is not a guarantee of class 2 membership, and several

Table 5.1 The main inflectional forms of Japanese verbs

		Negative
Non-past	*hanasu/miru*	*hanasanai/minai*
Past	*hanasita/mita*	*hanasanakatta/ minakatta*
Hortative	*hanasoo/miyoo*	
Imperative	*hanase/miro*	*hanasuna/miruna*
Stem	*hanasi/mi*	
Provisional	*hanaseba/mireba*	*hanasanakereba/ minakereba*
Conjunctive	*hanasite/mite*	*hanasanakute/ minakute, hanasanaide/minaide*
Conditional	*hanasitara/mitara*	*hanasanakattara/ minakattara*
Representative	*hanasitari/mitari*	*hanasanakattari/ minakattari*

common verbs of this shape (including *hairu* 'go in', *iru* 'be necessary', *kaeru* 'go (home, etc.)', *syaberu* 'talk') fall in class 1.

The main inflectional forms of Japanese verbs are illustrated in table 5.1, using *hanasu* 'speak' (class 1) and *miru* 'look at, see' (class 2) as representative verbs. Looking first at the forms, with class 1 verbs the basic rule is to subtract the final *-u* of the non-past and to add the relevant endings to the remainder as indicated: i.e. *hanas-(u)* + *-ita/-oo/-e/-i/-eba/-anai*, etc.; with class 2 verbs the rule is to subtract the final *-ru* and add the appropriate endings: i.e. *mi-* + *ta/-yoo/-ro/-ϕ* (i.e. 'zero')/*-reba/-nai*, etc. Class 1 verbs involve the additional complication that the precise shape of underlined forms (past/conjunctive/conditional/representative) varies according to the ending of the non-past:

Non–past	Past, etc.
-ku (e.g. *kaku* 'write')	*kaita (kaite, kaitara, kaitari)*
-gu (e.g. *oyogu* 'swim')	*oyoida*
-su (e.g. *hanasu* 'speak')	*hanasita*
-au/-uu/-ou/-tu/-ru (e.g. *kau* 'buy', *suu* 'inhale', *omou* 'think', *matu* 'wait', *noru* 'get in, on')	*katta/sutta/omotta/matta/ notta*
-nu/-bu/-mu (e.g. *sinu* 'die', *yobu* 'call', *yomu* 'read')	*siNda/yoNda/yoNda*

Negative forms of verbs inflect like *i* adjectives but feature the additional presence of negative imperative forms (non-past + *na*) and of *-naide* conjunctive forms. Class 1 verbs in *-au/-uu/-ou* add *-wanai* rather than *-anai* in the negative: *kau/suu/omou* give *kawanai/suwanai/omowanai*, etc. Other common English labels for our 'class 1'/'class 2' include '*-u* verbs'/'*-ru* verbs' (based on the non–past ending) and 'consonant verbs'/'vowel verbs' (based on the typical final sound of stems).

Irregular items in all languages tend to be common words. The two most thoroughly irregular verbs in Japanese are *suru* 'do' and *kuru* 'come':

Negative

Non-past	*suru/kuru*	*sinai/konai*, etc.
Past	*sita/kita*	
Hortative	*siyoo/koyoo*	
Imperative	*siro/koi*	
Stem	*si/ki*	
Provisional	*sureba/kureba*	

Some other verbs basically follow class 1 but with individual irregularities. A small group of special subject-honorific verbs ending in -*aru* (*irassyaru* 'be located (of animates), go, come', *nasaru* 'do', *ossyaru* 'say, be called', *kudasaru* 'give (to me/us, etc.)') have imperatives ending in -*ai* (*irassyai/nasai/ossyai/kudasai*) rather than the expected -*are* (**irassyare*, etc.). In addition, *irassyaru* has past and related forms *irasita*, etc. as common alternatives to expected *irassyatta*. The verb *iku* 'go' has past and related forms *itta*, etc. rather than **iita*. *Yuu* 'say, be called' behaves as if its non-past form were **iu* (and, indeed, it is so written in kana); other forms are *itta*, *ioo*, *ie*, *ii*, *ieba*, *iwanai*, etc., although past and related forms *yutta*, etc. are also used in speech. *Aru* 'be located (of inanimates)' has negative forms *nai*, etc. rather than expected **aranai*. Finally, *kureru* 'give (to me/us, etc.)' basically follows class 2 but has imperative *kure* rather than **kurero*.

Automatic control of inflections is fundamental to both production and comprehension in foreign language-learning, and they call for careful study and practice from the earliest stages. While the approach is not generally established for Japanese, there is a good deal to be said for learning verbs initially in several common principal forms, particularly for class 1; these might include non-past, past (or conjunctive), stem and negative (thus *kaku/kaita/kaki/kakanai* ('write'), *matu/ matta/mati/matanai* ('wait'), etc.). This would add some labour to the early stages of learning, but it would also serve to establish the patterns, which after all have to be mastered sooner or later.

Turning to the labels and uses of the forms, the main division is between the first four forms (non-past/past/horta-tive/imperative) and the rest. The first four forms are finite forms, in the sense that they may appear alone as predicates in simple sentences. Dictionary forms of Japanese verbs are commonly labelled 'non-past' rather than 'present' since their primary reference is to future (or habitual) actions and events: *NihoNgo de kaku* '(I)'ll write (it) in Japanese'/'(I) (always) write in Japanese'. However, with stative verbs reference is to present (or habitual) states: *Ka ga iru* 'There is a mosquito (here)'. Other common terms for our 'non-past' and 'past' are 'imperfect' and 'perfect'. The basic meaning of the hortative form—which has no negative counterpart—is 'let's (do)': *NihoNgo de kakoo* 'Let's write in Japanese'. Except with special subject-honorific verbs, imperatives are rare outside male in-formal speech. As we have seen, both hortatives (in their basic intentional meaning) and imperatives are found only with volitional verbs.

The remaining forms are non-finite and occur only in subordinate clauses or in combination with finite forms. One use of the stem form (sometimes called the 'infinitive') in spoken Japanese is in certain types of purpose clauses (*tabe ni iku* 'go to eat', *asobi ni kuru* 'come to visit'), and it also serves as the base for certain endings, notably in formal-style forms (*kakimasu*, etc.); it too has no negative counterpart. The basic meaning of the provisional form is 'provided that' or, in the negative, 'unless': *NihoNgo de kakeba ii* 'It's OK provided that (you) write in Japanese, i.e. (You) should write in Japanese'. The conjunctive form (sometimes called the 'gerund', the 'participial' form or the '-te form'—although it ends in -de in some cases) appears widely in coordinate and subordinate clauses where it corresponds roughly to English *and* (*Gozi ni okite tegami o kaita* '(I) got up at five o'clock and wrote a letter') and in combination with auxiliary verbs (*kaite iru* 'be writing', *kaite kureru* 'write (for me/us, etc.)'). Of the negative counterparts, *-naide* forms occur mainly with volitional verbs; they combine with auxiliaries (*Kakanaide kudasai* 'Please don't write') and occur elsewhere with the meanings 'without doing', 'rather than doing' (*GohaN o tabenaide dete itta* '(They) went out without eating', *NihoNgo de kakanaide eego de kakoo* 'Let's write (it) in English rather than writing (it) in Japanese'). In informal speech, both *-te/-de* and *-naide* forms appear alone as mild imperatives (cf. *Tyotto matte* 'Wait a minute', *Yamete* 'Stop (it)', *Iwanaide* 'Don't tell (them)', etc.); exceptionally, this is a finite use, which has doubtless arisen through the ellipsis of auxiliaries. Conditional forms are generally translated by 'if' or 'when': *Ame ga huttara doo siyoo?* 'What shall we do if it rains?', *GohaN o tabetara ikoo* 'Let's go when (we)'ve eaten'. Finally, representative forms (sometimes labelled 'alternative') occur either singly or in series in combination with the verb *suru* or the copula. They present an action, event, etc. as one occurrence among others (*Ame ga huttari yaNdari site iru* 'It's raining and stopping, i.e. It's raining off and on', *Tegami o kaitari hoN o yoNdari site ita* '(I) was writing letters, reading books, and such like').

I adjectives
Unlike verbs, *i* adjectives fall into a single inflectional class. They also show a smaller range of inflections:

Negative

Non-past	*hurui*	*huruku nai*
Past	*hurukatta*	*huruku nakatta*
-ku	*huruku*	
Conjunctive	*hurukute*	*huruku nakute*
Provisional	*hurukereba*	*huruku nakereba*
Conditional	*hurukattara*	*huruku nakattara*
Representative	*hurukattari*	*huruku nakattari*

As shown, *i* adjectives have fewer finite forms, lacking a hortative and imperative. As with verbs, 'non-past'/'past' are sometimes labelled 'imperfect'/'perfect'; also, 'non-past' is sometimes labelled 'present', with some justification since in the case of adjectives this form normally refers to present qualities or states. The -*ku* form is variously called the 'stem', 'infinitive' or 'adverbial form'. Its main uses are in combination with *nai* in negatives, as shown, and with verbs such as *suru* 'make', *naru* 'become' and *kaNziru* 'feel' (*ookiku suru* 'make big(ger), enlarge', *huruku naru* 'become old', *huruku kaNziru* 'feel as old'). As illustrated, negative forms involve combination with *nai*, which itself inflects as an *i* adjective. The only irregular *i* adjective is *ii* 'good, OK'; this has an irregular non-past form, all other endings being added to the inflectional stem *yo-* rather than *i-* (*yokatta/yoku/yokereba*, etc.). (The non-past form *yoi* also occurs in written Japanese.)

Copula

The copula—which corresponds roughly to the English verb 'to be' in its equative sense (*This is a book*, etc.)—is the remaining inflected word in Japanese. It is a grammatical word that is unique both in inflection and in wider grammatical behaviour and thus constitutes a special word class in its own right.

		Negative
Non-past	*da (no, na, φ) /de aru*	*zyanai/de nai*
Past	*datta /de atta*	*zyanakatta/de nakatta*
Conjunctive	*de /de atte*	*zyanakute/de nakute*
Provisional	*nara /de areba*	*zyanakereba/de nakereba*
Conditional	*dattara /de attara*	*zyanakattara/de nakattara*
Representative	*dattari /de attari*	*zyanakattari/de nakattari*

As we shall see, the non-past ('imperfect'/'present') form *da* is a troublesome form in Japanese grammar, which is replaced by *no* or *na* when it occurs before nouns and is also dropped (or 'replaced by zero') in certain cases, as in questions: *Kiree da* 'It's beautiful/clean', but *Kiree?* 'Is it beautiful/clean?' Historically, the copula has developed from the combination of *de* plus the verb *aru*, and the 'long' alternative forms appear in certain circumstances, notably with intervening range particles (thus *de wa aru*, *de mo atta*, *de mo nai*, etc.). Let us note also that the copula has a subject-honorific counterpart in *de irassyaru* '(RP) is ... ' and, as we have seen, an extra-formal equivalent in *de gozaimasu*: *SumisuseNsee wa amerikaziN de irassyaru* 'Professor Smith is an American', *Soo de gozaimasu* 'That is correct'. A most important feature of the copula is that it always occurs preceded by another word with which it is pronounced together as a single phrase like a particle: the response to *SumisusaN wa amerikaziN datta?* 'Was Smith an American?' must be *Soo datta* '(He) was so' rather than simply **Datta* '(He) was'.

Grammatical words

Grammatical words belong in closed sets: they may form special grammatical word classes (like the copula, various types of 'particles', etc.), or alternatively constitute grammatical subclasses of the major word classes (like auxiliary verbs). In general they are of basic importance in the construction of sentences and involve the most frequently used words in the language.

Demonstratives, interrogatives and indefinites

Demonstrative words (like English *this/that*, *here/there*) serve to identify things, places, etc., typically in terms of their location (*this book*: 'the book near the speaker', etc.); interrogative words (*what?/which?/where?*) seek identification; and indefinite words (*something/anything*, *somewhere/anywhere*) indicate a general category ('thing', 'place') but leave identity unspecified. Thus they share some common semantic ground, and in many languages they are also formally related.

Table 5.2 Major demonstrative and interrogative words

	ko- 'this (near me')'	so- 'that (near you')'	a- 'that (over there)'	do- 'which?'
Thing noun	kore 'this thing'	sore	are	dore 'which thing (of a selection)?'
Thing/ direction noun	kotira/kotti 'this thing (of two), this direction'	sotira/sotti	atira/atti	dotira/dotti
Place noun	koko 'this place'	soko	asoko/asuko	doko
Article	kono 'this'	sono	ano	dono 'which (of a selection)?'
Article	kooyuu 'of this nature'	sooyuu	aayuu	dooyuu
Adjective	koNna 'like this, of this degree'	soNna	aNna	doNna 'like what?, what sort of?'
Degree adverb	koNnani 'to this degree'	soNnani	aNnani	doNnani
Manner adverb	koo	soo	aa	doo

Japanese has a set of demonstrative and interrogative words that exhibit clear formal and semantic parallelism, and on this basis it is convenient to treat them together, although they straddle various word classes. The main items are shown in table 5.2.

The first point to note here is that Japanese has a three-way division among demonstratives (*ko-/so-/a-*), as opposed to a two-way division in English (*this/that*), with the contrast lying essentially in the fact that Japanese has two ways of saying 'that'. The basic distinction when one is referring to objects, etc. that are physically present in the situation is as indicated: *so-* words refer to objects close to the addressee ('that (near you)'); *a-* words to objects removed from both speaker and addressee ('that (over there)'): *Sono syasiN wa doko de totta?* 'Where did (you) take that photograph (which you are holding, etc.)?'/*Ano syasiN wa doko de totta?* 'Where did (you) take that photograph (over there on the wall, etc.)?'. When referring to things that are not actually present, *so-* is usual, unless the referent is regarded as being well known to both parties, when *a-* is used: *Konaida syasiN o totta N da kedo, sono syasiN no naka ni* . . . '(I) took some photos recently and among those (*so-*) photos . . . ', *Konaida totta syasiN wa doko? Are wa arubamu ni hatte oita yo* 'Where are those photos (we) took recently?' '(I) put those (*a-*) in the album'.

Secondly, these items span various word classes. *Kore* 'this thing' and *kotira/kotti* 'this thing (of two)/this direction', etc. are nouns; note that *kotira/kotti*, not *kore*, must be used where only two objects are involved: *Kore ni siyoo* 'I'll have this one (of three or more)'/*Kotti ni siyoo* 'I'll have this one (of two)'. *Kotira* and *kotti* differ in style, with the *kotti* series common in informal speech. *Koko* 'this place', etc. are also nouns, unlike their English translation equivalents *here/there*. Note that *asoko/asuko* are formally irregular (**ako* being the expected form); of the two, *asuko* is more informal. *Kono* 'this', etc. are articles and occur only before (modified or unmodified) nouns: *kono syasiN* 'this photograph', *ano siroi kuruma* 'that white car (over there)'. They are sometimes termed 'adnouns' or 'prenouns'.

Kooyuu 'of this nature' and *koNna* 'like this, of this degree' differ grammatically in that *kooyuu*, etc. are articles, while the *koNna* series also occur predicatively (*Uti wa koNna da kara . . .* 'Since our home is like this . . .'); this usage is somewhat uncommon, however. Both *koNna* and *kooyuu* roughly translate English *this kind/sort of* but they are definitely not synonymous, *koNna* being more impressionistic and, often, evaluative. *KoNnani*, etc. are degree adverbs and modify verbs and adjectives: *KoNnani komu to omowanakatta* '(I) didn't think it would get this crowded', *SoNnani muzukasiku nai* '(It)'s not that difficult'. The manner adverbs *koo*, etc. are particularly common in combination with the copula and such verbs as *naru* 'become', *suru* 'do', *yuu* 'say', *omou* 'think': *Soo da* '(That)'s right', *soo suru* 'do that', *soo yuu* 'say so, say that', *soo omou* 'think so'.

Finally, the use of the interrogative terms generally parallels that of the demonstratives but, as indicated, the noun *dore* 'which thing?' and the article *dono* 'which?' are used largely with reference to a given selection of objects, persons etc.: *Dore ga ii?* 'Which one (of the things here) is best?', *SuzukisaN wa dono hito?* 'Which person (in the photograph, etc.) is Suzuki?'

Basic interrogative terms outside the above series of terms include *dare* 'who?', *nani* (*naN* before *n*, *t*, *d*) 'what?', *itu* 'when?' Common conversational equivalents to 'why?' are *doosite* and *naNde*, and *dooyatte* 'how?' is also frequent in conversation.

Indefinite nouns are generally formed from interrogative nouns by the suffixation of *-ka*. Thus: *doreka* 'some one thing (of a selection)', *dotiraka* 'some one thing (of two)', *dokoka/* (informal) *dokka* 'somewhere', *dareka* 'someone', *nanika* 'something', *ituka* 'sometime'.

Quantifiers

Quantifiers are words that express quantity, either in a general way (*zeNbu* 'all', *hotoNdo* 'almost all', *takusaN* 'a lot, much') or numerically (*hutari* 'two (people)', *saNmai* 'three (flat objects)'). Numerical words like *hutari*, *saNmai* are usually termed 'numbers', and they are composed of two elements, a numeral (*huta-* 'two', *saN* 'three') plus a classifier (*-ri*, *-mai*). Unlike in English, where numerals are used as they stand to quantify words (*two people*, *three sheets*, etc.), Japanese numerals are not generally used as independent words. In considering numbers we must therefore look at numerals, at classifiers and at the mechanics of their combination, all of which involve some complexity.

First, numerals. Two striking features here are the presence of two distinct sets of numerals (with some variants) from one to ten, and the status of 10 000, rather than 1000, as the base for higher numerals (see table 5.3). Japanese numerals are

Table 5.3 Japanese numerals

1	*iti*	*hito-*
2	*ni*	*huta-*
3	*saN*	*mi-*
4	*si/yoN/yo-*	*yo-*
5	*go*	*itu-*
6	*roku*	*mu-*
7	*siti/nana*	*nana-*
8	*hati*	*ya-*
9	*ku/kyuu*	*kokono-*
10	*zyuu*	*too*
11	*zyuuiti*	
20	*nizyuu*	
100	*hyaku*	
1 000	*seN*	
10 000	*itimaN*	
100 000	*zyuumaN*	
1 000 000	*hyakumaN*	
10 000 000	*isseNmaN*	
100 000 000	*itioku*	
1 000 000 000 000	*ittyoo*	

Sino-Japanese in origin, with the exception of the alternative one–ten series (*hito-*, etc.), which are native. *YoN/yo-* (four) and *nana* (seven) originate in the native series but do duty as variants for SJ *si* and *siti*, which have the disadvantage of being phonetically similar. The basic principles of formation of higher numerals are straightforward (eleven = 'ten one', twenty = 'two ten', etc.), but are complicated by the presence of variants and by sound changes accompanying composition (*saN* + *hyaku* → *saNbyaku* (300), *roku* + *hyaku* → *roppyaku* (600), etc.); these resemble the normal changes in SJ binary words but show certain irregularities peculiar to numerals. As indicated, Japanese has a numerical unit for 10 000 (*maN*), and 10 000, rather than 1000, serves as the base for higher numerals: 100 000 is *zyuumaN* ('10 *maN*'), 1 000 000 is *hyakumaN* ('100 *maN*'), 10 000 000 is *isseNmaN* ('1 000 *maN*') and 100 000 000 is *itioku* ('1 *oku*' = 1 *maN* × 1 *maN*). The next higher unit, *-tyoo*, is 1 *maN* × 1 *oku* (1 000 000 000 000, i.e. one million million). Needless to say, mastery of this system requires considerable practice, but *maN-* and, to some degree, *oku*-sized numerals are frequently used in everyday life in referring to prices in yen.

In general, numerals are only used independently in purely numerical contexts (e.g. in counting on one's fingers, in mathematics, etc.). To count things, they must be combined with classifiers to form number words. A relatively small set of classifiers are in everyday use, of which the most common include the following: *-ri/-niN* (persons), *-too* (horses, cows, etc.), *-hiki* (animals: general), *-satu* (books), *-dai* (vehicles, machines), *-keN* (buildings), *-hoN* (elongated things), *-mai* (flat things), *-ko* (smallish, solid things), *-tu* (things: general). Different classifiers are used to count different entities, either in terms of their specific identity (as persons, animals, books, etc.) or, in the case of many inanimate objects, in terms of their shape. Of the 'shape' classifiers, *-hoN* is used to count trees, fingers, cigarettes, bottles, teeth, roads, etc., as well as more abstract elongated entities such as bus services and telephone calls; *-mai* is used for plates, records, blankets, coins and bank-notes, playing cards, tickets, sheets of paper, etc., and *-ko* for apples, eggs, etc. The general classifier *-tu* is used for things that lie outside the range of these more specific items.

Virtually all the classifiers above combine with SJ numerals. With the expected complications arising from variants and sound changes, these combinations result in numbers such as *yoniN* 'four (people)', *issatu* 'one (book)', *zyuppoN/zippoN* 'ten (elongated things)', *rokko* 'six (solid things'), etc. Exceptionally, the general classifier *-tu* and the person classifier *-ri* combine with native numerals. *-tu* numbers have sound changes involving the gemination of *t* with one-syllable numerals: the *-tu* numerals from one to nine are *hitotu/hutatu/mittu/yottu/itutu/muttu/nanatu/yattu/kokonotu*; *too* 'ten' is used as a number in its own right. (Above ten, general things are counted simply with SJ numerals: *zyuuiti* 'eleven (general things)', etc.). *-ri* combines only with *hito-* and *huta-*, producing *hitori* 'one (person)' and *hutari* 'two (people)'. Interrogative numbers ('how many?') are formed with *naN-* in the case of SJ classifiers (*naNniN* 'how many (people)?', *naNgeN* 'how many (buildings)?', *naNmai* 'how many (flat things)?', etc.), and with *iku-* for native classifiers (*ikutu* 'how many (general things)?'.)

Numerals also combine with measures to form measure words which in many respects resemble numbers. Common measures include the following:

Money:	*-eN* 'yen', *-doru* 'dollars'
Length, distance:	*-seNti* 'centimetres', *meetoru* 'metres', *-kiro* 'kilometres'
Weight:	*-guramu* 'grams', *-kiro* 'kilograms'
Time:	*-zikaN* 'hours', *-ka(kaN)/-niti(kaN)* 'days', *-syuukaN* 'weeks', *-kagetu (kaN)* 'months', *-neN(kaN)* 'years'
Volume:	*-hai* 'spoonfuls, cupfuls, glassfuls'

Again, combination is normally with SJ numerals, except with days where *-ka* combines with native numerals, with the expected irregularities (cf. *hutuka* 'two days'/*muika* 'six days'/ *nanoka* 'seven days'/*yooka* 'eight days'). Interrogative measure words are formed in the usual way (*naNniti* 'how many days?', *naNbai* 'how many cupfuls?' etc.), but 'how much (money)?' is *ikura*. A common general interrogative word in this area is *donogurai* ('about how much/how long, etc.?').

Quantifiers are generally viewed as a subclass of nouns. While they may in certain cases be followed by *ga* or *o*, they commonly occur in sentences directly before the verb (cf. *Rekoodo o nimai katta* '(I) bought two records') or linked to head nouns with *no* (cf. *Sono nimai no rekoodo o katta* '(I) bought those two records').

Auxiliaries

Auxiliaries are grammatical verbs that combine with the conjunctive form of main (lexical) verbs to express notions relating primarily to the aspect and directionality of the action or event described. All the auxiliaries also occur in their own right as lexical verbs—as verbs of location, placement and change of location, verbs of seeing, and verbs of giving and receiving. Many of these verbs have special honorific and/or extraformal counterparts and, importantly, these are also used as auxiliaries.

The first auxiliary, *iru*, has already been discussed in relation to the aspectual division of verbs into dynamic and stative: *iru* combines with dynamic verbs to express action in progress or resultant state, depending on the subclass of the verb. With action verbs (such as *taberu* 'eat') action in progress is the usual meaning, whereas with change-of-state verbs (such as *tukareru* 'become tired') reference is to resultant state. Subject-honorific *irassyaru* and extra-formal *orimasu* regularly appear as auxiliaries, as in *tabete irassyaru* '(RP) is eating', *tukarete irassyaru* '(RP) is tired' and *Ame ga hutte orimasu* 'It is raining'.

Auxiliary *aru* (extra-formal *gozaimasu*), a verb of location like *iru*, expresses the existence of a state resulting from the action of the main verb. It combines with transitive volitional verbs, as in *katte aru* 'has been bought (by someone)', *akete aru* 'has been opened (by someone)'. This resembles the resultative meaning of *iru*, but with *aru* there is a clear implication that an actor has been involved, with a deliberate purpose. In *Mado ga simete aru* 'The windows have been closed (by someone)', with *aru*, the focus is on the fact that the windows have been (deliberately) closed by someone (often the speaker); in *Mado ga simatte iru*, with *iru* and an intransitive change-of-state verb, the focus is simply on the state of the windows, with no concern for how that state might have arisen.

As a main verb, *oku* means 'put, place (something somewhere)'; putting an object somewhere results in that object being located (*aru*) there, and a semantic link is discernible between the auxiliary uses of these two verbs. Like *aru*, *oku* combines with volitional verbs, and its basic meaning might be expressed as 'do something so that the result of the action exists'—i.e. the focus is not so much on the nature of the action as such, but on deliberately getting the action done for the sake of its result. Perhaps the clearest situation of this type is when an action is done in preparation for some anticipated eventuality and, as we have seen, this is a common meaning for auxiliary *oku*. A related meaning is 'leave (something in its present state)'; out of context, *Mado o simete okoo* may mean 'Let's close the windows (in anticipation of rain, etc.)' or 'Let's leave the windows closed (as they are)', and only the situation will indicate which meaning is intended.

As a lexical verb, *simau* is a verb of placement or disposal meaning 'put away' (cf. *hutoN o osiire ni simau* 'put the bedding away in the closet'), and as an auxiliary it combines with dynamic verbs with two common meanings. The first is that an action or event occurs to the point of finality: *tabete simau* 'eat up, eat (it) all', *kiete simau* 'disappear completely, vanish without trace', *sugite simau* '(something) passes, becomes over and done with'. Secondly, it is used to indicate an unexpected or unwanted action or event outside one's control: *Terebi ga kowarete simatta* 'The TV has (gone and) broken down', *Ano hito ni yutte simatta* 'I (went and) told him/ended up telling him (although I didn't intend to)'. As we shall see later, *-te/-de simau* have given rise to the contractions *-tyau/-zyau*, which are widely used in spoken Japanese.

The basic verbs of change-of-location, *kuru* 'come' and *iku* 'go' (with shared subject-honorific *irassyaru* and extra-formal *mairimasu*), both occur as auxiliaries with several uses. The most literal uses involve physical motion, as with the lexical verbs: *tabete kuru* means 'come, having eaten', and it is used where in English we would say 'eat before coming, eat on the way (here)', or 'go and eat (and come back)'. Similarly, *tabete iku* means 'go, having eaten', i.e. 'eat before going'. In more figurative uses, *kuru* presents an event or change as impinging on the speaker: *Ame ga hutte kita* 'It's come on to rain', *Onaka ga suite kita* '(My) stomach has come to be empty, i.e. I'm feeling hungry', *Muzukasiku natte kita* '(It)'s become difficult'; this usage is very common in spoken Japanese. *Iku*, by contrast, indicates a progressive development that is presented as proceeding away from the speaker, often into the future: *ikite iku* 'live, make one's way through life', *huete iku* 'go on increasing', etc.

Miru 'look at, see' is used as an auxiliary with the clearly related meaning '(do something and) see (what happens, how it feels, etc.)'. It combines with volitional action verbs: *yatte miru* 'do (something) and see, have a go at (something)', *kite miru* 'put on and see, try on', *mite miru* 'have a look and see', *tabete miru* 'eat and see, try'.

The remaining auxiliaries are basically verbs of giving and receiving and may collectively be referred to as 'benefactives'. They are used to express the fact that a (volitional) action is performed for the benefit of someone, and their presence may be seen as a reflection of the Japanese cultural concern with relations of benefaction and indebtedness. As we have seen, Japanese has two lexical verbs of giving, *kureru* (subject-honorific *kudasaru*) and *ageru* (object-honorific *sasiageru*), distinguished in terms of the direction of the giving relative to the speaker; this distinction is maintained in the auxiliary uses. Thus, *katte kureru* '(someone) buys (for me/us, etc.)', *kite kureru* '(someone) comes (as a favour to me/us)', *homete kureru* '(someone) praises (me/us)' vs *katte ageru* '(I/we, etc.) buy (for someone)', *itte ageru* '(I/we) go (as a favour to someone/on someone's behalf)', *homete ageru* '(I/we) praise (someone)'. As a lexical verb *morau* (object-honorific *itadaku*) means '(I/we, etc.) receive, get, be given', and it is also commonly used as an auxiliary, meaning '(I/we) receive the favour of (someone doing something for us), (I/we etc.) have (someone do something for us)': *katte morau* '(I/we) have (something) bought (for us)', *kite morau* '(I/we) get (someone) to come', *homete morau* '(I/we) receive praise (from someone)'.

Benefactives sometimes cause problems for English-speaking learners. At a general level, Japanese tends to express these notions much more widely than English, so that there is a tendency for learners to omit them: 'My friend invited me' is naturally expressed in Japanese as *Tomodati ga yoNde kureta*, not as *Tomodati ga yoNda*, which leaves the Japanese listener wondering what was objectionable about the invitation. More particularly, the common benefactive use of *morau* often presents initial difficulties. It is important to see that this is a natural extension of its basic lexical use; just as one may receive a gift, so one may receive a favour from someone, and indeed English uses the verb *get* in a not dissimilar way (cf. *get a guitar for Christmas/get someone to do something for me*).

Particles

The term 'particle' is generally used to refer to small, un-inflected grammatical words in Japanese that follow the items to which they relate and are normally pronounced together with preceding material. Despite these common features, they fall into several quite different groups in terms of their function, and it is extremely important to distinguish clearly between these.

Case markers

Case markers follow nouns (or noun phrases, i.e., broadly, modified nouns) and indicate the relation of these nouns to the following verb or other predicate.

We are already familiar with the notion of the 'valency' of a verb: a given verb describes a particular type of situation and typically 'expects' a number of central associated nouns referring to different types of participants or other aspects of the situation (actors, destinations, etc.). These central nouns are generally indicated by the core case markers *ga*, *o* and *ni*, depending on the type of verb.

Verbs with a valency of one mark the associated noun with *ga*: *ame ga huru* 'rain falls', *terebi ga kowareru* 'the television breaks down', *sode ga nagasugiru* 'sleeves are too long', etc. Depending on the meaning of the verb, these nouns refer to actors (*ame*), entities which undergo changes of state (*terebi*) or entities which are in a given state (*sode*).

Verbs with a valency of two mark one associated noun with *ga* and the other most generally with *o* or *ni*. *Ga* and *o* typically occur where a human or other animate agent (*ga*) effects some kind of a change on an entity (*o*): *kodomo ga terebi o kowasu* 'the child breaks the television', *neko ga sakana o taberu* 'the cat eats the fish', etc.; also where an entity (*o*) is newly produced, is manipulated or is actively perceived: *gakusee ga gohaN o tukuru* 'the student makes the meal', *inu ga sippo o huru* 'the dog wags (its) tail', *kodomo ga terebi o miru* 'the child watches television', etc. *Ga* and *ni* occur, firstly, where a person or thing (*ga*) is located in a given place (*ni*): *koko ni hoN ga aru* 'there is a book here', *kodomo ga nikai ni iru* 'the child is upstairs', *okaasaN ga tookyoo ni suNde iru* 'the mother lives in Tokyo'; also where a person, etc. (*ga*) changes to a new location (*ni*; *e* also occurs here): *syatyoo ga oosaka ni iku* 'the president goes to Osaka', *neko ga soto ni deru* 'the cat goes outside', *kodomo ga kuruma ni noru* 'the child gets in the car'. They are also found where a person or entity (*ga*) encounters or collides with another (*ni*): *gakusee ga tomodati ni au* 'the student meets a friend', *booru ga piN ni ataru* 'the ball hits the flagstick', or is transformed into a new condition (*ni*): *oyu ga mizu ni naru* 'the hot water becomes cold water'. Finally, *ga* and *ni* occur in certain circumstances with verbs such as *iru* 'be necessary', *wakaru* 'be understandable', *mieru* 'be visible', where *ni* marks the possessor/experiencer: *okaasaN ni okane ga iru* 'the mother needs money', *ano hito ni doitugo ga wakareba* 'provided that he/she understands German', etc.

Verbs with a valency of three generally combine *ga*, *o* and *ni*. As with bivalent verbs, *ni* is used to indicate a changed location (*e* also occurs here) (e.g. *okaasaN ga neko o soto ni dasu* 'the mother puts the cat outside'), an entity which is encountered or collided with (*kodomo ga tukue ni asi o butukeru* 'the child bangs its leg on the desk'), or an entity transformed into a new condition (*kodomo ga koko o beNkyoobeya ni suru* 'the child makes this place into a study'). *Ni* also marks the recipient of an entity (*okaasaN ga kodomo ni omotya o ageru* 'the mother gives the child a toy'), the receiver of an act of communication (*kodomo ga omawarisaN ni miti o kiku* 'the child asks the policeman the way') and the beneficiary of an action (*okaasaN ga kodomo ni omotya o kau*) 'the mother buys a toy for the child'). With verbs of acquisition, *ni* marks the person *from* whom the entity is acquired (although *kara* also occurs here): *kodomo ga okaasaN ni omotya o morau* 'the child receives a toy from the mother', *kodomo ga tomodati ni hoN o kariru* 'the child borrows a book from the friend'.

As indicated, in addition to *ga/o/ni*, *e* ('to': destination) and *kara* ('from': source) sometimes mark core cases. This also applies to *to* (reciprocal), which commonly marks the second party with verbs which describe a mutual action, process or relation: *A ga B to kekkoNsuru* 'A marries B', *A ga B to wakareru* 'A parts from B', *A ga B to tigau* 'A is different from B'; *to* may replace *ni* with verbs such as *au* 'see (and talk with), meet' and *hanasu* 'talk' (*A ga B to C o hanasu* 'A talks over C with B') where the encounter or interaction is presented as two-way.

Remaining uses of case markers generally involve more peripheral nouns, that is to say, nouns that occur as optional extras rather than being logically necessary to complete the sense of the verb. *Kara* ('from, since') typically follows place or time nouns (*tookyoo kara nimotu o okuru* 'send luggage from Tokyo', *kyoneN kara nihoN ni iru* 'have been in Japan since

last year'), as does *made* ('as far as, to, until'): *eki made aruku*
'walk to the station', *ohiru made uti ni iru* 'be at home
until midday'. These two items often occur together, marking
beginning and end points: *nizi kara yozi made kaisya ni iru*
'be at the office from two until four'. *De* is a common case
marker that marks a variety of semantic relations, notably
scene of action or event following place nouns (*kooeN de asobu*
'play in the park'), instrument or medium (*omotya de asobu*
'play with toys', *razio de kiku* 'hear on the radio') and non-
human cause (*kaze de taoreru* 'fall over due to the wind, be
blown down by the wind'). *To* (comitative: 'in company
with') marks a human or animal companion: *inu to asobu* 'play
with the dog', *tomodati to ryokoosuru* 'travel with a friend'. Core
markers also have some peripheral uses: *o* occurs with verbs of
motion or change of location marking place nouns as path (*miti
o aruku* 'walk along the road', *koosateN o magaru* 'turn at/
through the intersection') or as source (*heya o deru* 'go out of
the room', *kuruma o oriru* 'get out of the car'), and *ni* follows
certain time nouns as a marker of point of time: *zyuuzi ni neru*
'go to bed at ten o'clock', *kugatu ni amerika ni iku* 'go to
America in September'. (Other, less specific time nouns normally occur without case markers in this use: *raineN amerika
ni iku* 'go to America next year', etc.) *Madeni* is a time marker
that combines *made* 'until' and *ni* 'at (a specific time)'; it
corresponds to English 'by' and occurs following time nouns
with volitional verbs: *asita madeni kaeru* 'return (home, etc.) by
tomorrow'.

Adjectives also have valencies. The majority are mono-
valent and, as with verbs, they mark the associated noun with
ga: *niwa ga hiroi* 'garden is spacious', *me ga akai* 'eyes are red',
karada ga ookii 'body is big', etc. Some are bivalent and, unlike
with verbs, the second noun is never marked by *o*. Instead, we
commonly find *ni* (*okaasaN ga kodomo ni amai* 'the mother is
indulgent to children'), *to* (*are ga kore to onazi da (kara)* '(since)
that is the same as this', *satoosaN ga suzukisaN to sitasii (kara)*
'(since) Sato is friendly with Suzuki') and *ga* (for example, with
adjectives relating to liking, wanting and capability: *kodomo*

ga niku ga kirai da (kara) '(since) the child dislikes meat', *watasi ga kuruma ga hosii (kara)* '(since) I want a car', *tomodati ga goruhu ga zyoozu da (kara)* '(since) the friend is good at golf'). *Ni* is also common as a peripheral marker, often corresponding to English 'for': *tabako ga karada ni warui (kara)* '(since) cigarettes are bad for the health', *koko ga kaimono ni hubeN da (kara)* '(since) this place is inconvenient for shopping', etc. *Yori* 'compared with' commonly occurs with adjectives (and certain verbs) in comparative sentences: *Atti yori kotti ga ii* 'This one is good compared with that one, i.e. This is better than that', etc.

A few Japanese verbs and adjectives have a valency of zero, i.e. do not require any additional items to round out their sense. The most obvious examples are words such as *harumeku* 'become spring-like' and *kurai* 'dark', referring to natural environmental processes and states. We should also point out that valency slots need not always be filled by nouns: a verb such as *naru* 'become', for example, requires an item referring to a resulting condition, and while this slot may be occupied by a noun (marked by *ni*), it may also be filled by an adjective (in the *-ku* form if inflected, followed by *ni* if uninflected): *huruku naru* 'become old', *kiree ni naru* 'become beautiful/clean', *pikapika ni naru* 'become sparkling (clean)'.

Japanese case markers, at least the more peripheral ones, are often translated by English prepositions (*to, from, at, with*, etc.), and they are sometimes termed 'postpositions' since they follow nouns rather than precede them as in English. Needless to say, there are numerous mismatches between the two languages here. One of the most troublesome distinctions for English-speaking learners is that between locative uses of *ni* and *de*: broadly speaking, *ni* marks static location or resulting location following a change of state (i.e. it answers the question 'Where is a person/entity located?'), while *de* marks the scene of an activity ('Where does an action take place?'). English uses the same prepositions (*in, at*, etc.) here and does not distinguish between such pairs as *tookyoo de hoN o kau* 'buy a book in Tokyo'/*tookyoo ni ie o kau* 'buy a house in Tokyo' (i.e. the house is located in Tokyo) and *Kyooto ni otera ga takusaN aru* 'There are many temples (located) in Kyoto'/*Kyooto de omaturi ga takusaN aru* 'There are many festivals (performed) in Kyoto'.

A final case marker, *no* (genitive), stands somewhat apart in that it links nouns not to predicates but to other nouns: *watasi no kuruma* 'my car', *tookyoo no hoteru* 'Tokyo hotels', etc. Two points are of central importance in its use. Firstly, although the term 'genitive' primarily suggests a relation of possession, the semantic connection between the two nouns may be much wider than this: the basic meaning of N1 *no* N2 is rather 'N2 which is associated with N1'. Secondly, it is essential not to confuse the order of the two nouns. This follows the overriding principle of Japanese word order that modifiers precede the items which they modify (their 'heads'): *watasi no kuruma* thus refers to a kind of *kuruma*, namely *watasi no*, i.e. 'associated with me', etc. Compare the following examples, which further illustrate both these points: *ano hito no kuruma* 'his/her car', *kyoo no siNbuN* 'today's newspaper', *nihoN no siNbuN* 'newspapers in Japan', *nihoNgo no siNbuN* 'Japanese (-language) newspapers', *siNbuN no nihoNgo* 'Japanese language in newspapers, i.e. newspaper Japanese', *gomu no tebukuro* 'rubber gloves', *tebukuro no gomu* 'rubber in/of the gloves', *hako no naka* 'interior of the box', *naka no hako* 'the box (which is) inside', *kawa no mukoo* 'place beyond the river', *mukoo no kawa* 'river (which is) over there'.

Range markers

The two basic range markers are the particles *wa* and *mo*; they are sometimes termed 'focus particles', and *wa* is often referred to as a 'topic marker'. The use of *wa*, in particular, is one of the most difficult problems facing the English-speaking learner of Japanese.

The first requirement is to distinguish range markers clearly from case markers. In the first place, they appear in different positions. As we have seen, case markers follow nouns directly: *tookyoo e* 'to Tokyo', *tookyoo kara* 'from Tokyo', *tookyoo de* '(action performed) in Tokyo', etc. By contrast, range markers basically follow combinations of noun + case marker: *tookyoo e wa, tookyoo kara mo, tookyoo de wa*, etc. The one apparent exception to this—and this is one of the most important rules of Japanese grammar—is that the core case markers *ga, o* and (sometimes) *ni* are omitted in such combinations; in other words, expected **tookyoo ga wa*, **tookyoo o wa* and (sometimes) *tookyoo ni wa* all surface as *tookyoo wa*, and similarly with *mo*. Furthermore, range markers also occur, for example, after verbal, adjectival and copular forms (cf. *tukarete iru* 'be tired'/ *tukarete wa iru, huruku nai* 'not be old'/*huruku mo nai, de aru* 'is/are'/*de mo aru*, etc.). Thus they have a different and wider range of occurrence than case markers.

As we have seen, the function of case markers is to relate nouns semantically to the verb or other predicate that governs them: they indicate 'who did what to whom', 'who went where, how and when', etc. Range markers are quite independent of such notions. In a sentence such as *Kinoo satoosaN ga suzukisaN o koko de mita* 'Yesterday Sato saw Suzuki here', switching around case markers will result in the description of a different event or in an ungrammatical sentence. However, range markers may be freely introduced with no effect on these basic semantic relations: *Kinoo wa satoosaN ga suzukisaN o koko de mita/SatoosaN wa kinoo suzukisaN o koko de mita/SuzukisaN wa kinoo satoosaN ga koko de mita/Koko de wa kinoo satoosaN ga suzukisaN o mita* all describe the same basic event.

What, then, is the function of range markers? The simple, although unrevealing, answer is that they frame the information in a different way. *Mo* is the easier item to understand. It commonly corresponds to English 'also' or 'even', and *Kinoo mo satoosaN ga suzukisaN o koko de mita* means 'Yesterday (in addition to other days) Sato saw Suzuki here', *SatoosaN mo kinoo suzukisaN o koko de mita* 'Sato (in addition to other people) saw Suzuki here yesterday', etc. Essentially, *mo* indicates that the information given in the rest of the sentence applies to the word(s) marked by *mo in addition to* other items of the same kind. *Wa* is basically the opposite of *mo*: it indicates that the information in the rest of the sentence applies to the word(s) marked by *wa irrespective of* other items of the same kind: *Kinoo wa satoosaN ga suzukisaN o koko de mita* presents the information as applying to yesterday, in isolation from other items of the same kind (i.e. other days), *SuzukisaN wa kinoo satoosaN ga koko de mita* as applying to Suzuki, irrespective of other people, etc. Whereas *mo* marks an item as similar to others in the same range, *wa* marks an item as independent from others in the range: in this sense *mo* is inclusive or integrating, *wa* exclusive or segregating.

An understanding of the meaning of these markers in these terms does not automatically enable us to use them correctly. Especially in the case of *wa*, which has no general equivalent in English, it is useful to consider some characteristic uses in the light of this presentation. One common use of *wa* is to indicate the topic of a question containing interrogative words such as *dare* 'who?', *nani* 'what?', etc. As it stands, a 'bare' question such as *Nani o taberu?* 'What are (we) going to eat?' has no topic specified (although this may be clear from the situation—e.g. if one has just entered a restaurant, etc.). To ask 'What are we going to eat for dinner?', the natural Japanese equivalent is *YuuhaN wa nani o taberu?* where *yuuhaN* 'dinner' specifies the topic over which the question is to be understood as operating: 'I wish to ask about *yuuhaN* in isolation from other possibilities: What are we going to eat?' Compare other commonplace examples: *Saihu wa doko ni itta?* 'Where has my wallet gone?', *Basyo wa doko?* 'Where is the venue (for the meeting, party, etc.)?', *Kono hito wa dare?* 'Who is this person?' So characteristic is this use that *X wa?* (with rising intonation on *wa*) serves as a common formula for asking obvious questions: *OkaasaN wa?* 'Where's Mother?' etc., *Syokuzi wa?* 'How about (your) meal?, i.e. Have (you) eaten?', etc., *Kasa wa?* 'Where is (your) umbrella?' etc. In these cases the item marked by *wa* is typically selected from an unspecified range of other possible items: i.e. *YuuhaN wa nani o taberu* asks about *yuuhaN* and not about other possibilities, without there necessarily being any particular contrast implied (*yuuhan* as specifically opposed to *ohiru* 'lunch', etc.).

Given its segregating character, however, *wa* is also the natural marker to use where one is drawing contrasts between items from a specified range. Thus *wa* commonly appears where one is making contrasting statements about items from a similar range: *SumisusaN wa igirisuzin da kedo okusaN wa huraNsuziN da* 'Smith is British, but his wife is French', *Ame wa ooi kedo yuki wa huranai* 'Rain is plentiful, but snow doesn't fall, i.e. It rains a lot but it doesn't snow', *Kootya wa nomu kedo koohii wa nomanai* '(I) drink tea but (I) don't drink coffee'.

Wa is also common in negative sentences, where its effect is to specify the range of the negation and, often, by implication to play up a contrast with comparable positive states of affairs: 'I didn't do X (but I did do Y)', 'We don't have X (but we do have Y)', etc.: the straightforward negative response to *Koohii aru?* 'Is there any coffee' is simply *Nai* 'There isn't'; the response *Koohii wa nai* explicitly restricts the range of the negation to *koohii*, thereby suggesting that other comparable alternatives are available ('There isn't any coffee (but there is some tea)', etc.). Note that the usual negative forms of the copula historically incorporate *wa*, *zyanai* being a contraction of *de wa nai*, etc.

There are also characteristic situations where *wa* does not occur. Firstly, it is never used *following* interrogatives such as *dare* 'who?', *doko* 'what place?', etc. (although, as we have seen, it is commonly used to mark the topic of questions containing these words). Thus, *Dare ni atta?* 'Who did (you) meet?' (not **Dare ni wa atta?*), *Doko de taberu?* 'Where shall (we) eat? (not **Doko de wa taberu?*), etc. By extension, *wa* is not used with items that answer such questions: it is an important general principle that answers echo questions in their grammatical structure. Thus, *Natuyasumi wa doko ni iku?* 'Where shall (we) go for the summer holidays?' is answered by *Umi ni ikoo* 'Let's go to the seaside' (not **Umi ni wa ikoo*), *GohaN wa dare ga tukutta?* 'Who made the meals?' by *OziisaN ga tukutta* 'Granddad made (them)' (not **OziisaN wa tukutta*), etc. *Wa* also does not occur in 'out-of-the blue' descriptions, where the speaker reacts to newly cognized situations. On noticing that it has started to rain, one says *Ame ga hutte kita* 'It's started raining' (not *Ame wa hutte kita*), and on finding ants in one's kitchen one says *Ari ga iru* 'There are ants (here)' (not *Ari wa iru*). Note that such descriptions can been seen as answering the (implicit) questions 'What's happening?', 'What's going on?'

By contrast, statements that can be seen as answering questions posed about particular topics may contain *wa*. Thus, *NihoNgo ga muzukasii* and *NihoNgo wa muzukasii* 'Japanese is difficult' are both grammatical sentences. The first sentence is more restricted in use and would normally occur in response to a question such as *NihoNgo to doitugo to dotti ga muzukasii* 'Which is (more) difficult, Japanese or German?' The second serves rather as an answer to (implicit or explicit) questions such as *NihoNgo wa doo?* 'How is Japanese?' It is in relation to statements of this kind that *wa* is often said to mark the 'topic' (and we have used this term ourselves in relation to questions containing interrogatives), but this is valuable as an explanation only if we can specify independently what, precisely, a 'topic' is.

We have focused on examples where *wa* follows combinations of noun + case particle but, as noted at the beginning of this section, it also occurs in other positions, as in *Tukarete wa inai* '(I)'m not tired (but my eyes are sore, etc.)' in response to *Tukareta?* 'Are (you) tired?', *Huruku wa nai* '(It)'s not old (but it's pretty dilapidated, etc.)' in response to *Hurui?* 'Is it old?', where the explicit specification of the range serves to suggest the presence of some other comparable condition. *Wa* also occurs following quantifiers. For example, another possible answer to *Koohii aru?* 'Is there any coffee?' is *Sukosi aru* 'There is a little'. In *Sukosi wa aru* the range of the statement is restricted to the item *sukosi* 'a little' (i.e. 'In so far as we are talking about "a little", we have some'), giving rise to an implied contrast with other amounts ('a lot', etc.); the force is thus similar to English 'just a little'.

There is much more to be said about *wa*, and whole books could be—and indeed have been—devoted to the subject. As a learning item, it poses problems for English-speaking learners of a comparable order to the difficulties of English articles (*the/a*, etc.) for speakers of Japanese. Part of its difficulty clearly lies in the fact that it has no single close counterpart in English; indeed, many of the distinctions relevant to its use are expressed in English, not through grammar or vocabulary, but through stress and intonation, and the notions involved often appear accordingly elusive.

Our focus on *wa* has correspondingly restricted our discussion of *mo*, which, although more straightforward, is still worthy of attention. It has characteristic uses with quantifiers. Firstly, it appears in negative sentences following words denoting small amounts (*Sukosi mo nai* 'There isn't even a little, i.e. There is not at all', *Hitori mo konakatta* 'Not even one person came, i.e. No one at all came'); in positive sentences, it implies that the quantity marked is considered large (*ItizikaN matta* '(I) waited an hour'/*ItizikaN mo matta* '(I) waited as long as one hour'). Notice also that when it combines with the copula (i.e. when one wishes to say 'is/also X', 'isn't X, either'), it gives rise to the long forms *de mo aru*, *de mo nai*, etc.: cf. the common expression *Soo de mo nai kedo ne* 'It's not like that, either'.

How far the class of range markers should be extended beyond *wa* and *mo* is somewhat unclear; there are several other candidates, but they tend to exhibit some differences in grammatical behaviour from these central members. *Sika* 'except for' is a relatively clear case. This marker normally occurs only in negative sentences, and its translation equivalent is generally '(positive) + only'. As with *wa* and *mo*, it follows noun and case marker combinations, and *ga*, *o* and (sometimes) *ni* are omitted; however, it does not occur following verbal and adjectival forms. Compare *Kore sika nai* 'There is only this', *Tookyoo ni sika itte inai* '(We)'ve only been to Tokyo', *Sukosi sika nai* 'There is only a little', etc.

Illocutionary markers

Illocutionary markers are particles that are added, generally at the ends of sentences, to indicate the force of an utterance, i.e. whether the speaker is asking a question, putting forward an assertion, seeking confirmation, etc. They may also reflect other aspects of the speech situation, including the gender of the speaker, and they are a characteristic feature of spoken Japanese. They are often referred to as '(sentence-)final particles'.

The first illocutionary marker, *ka*, indicates that the sentence to which it is added is uttered as a question: *Ikoo* 'Let's go'/*Ikoo ka* 'Shall we go?', etc. In informal speech, questions ending in non-past and past forms are commonly indicated simply by rising intonation: *Ikanai?* 'Aren't (you) going to go?', *Omosiroi?* 'Is (it) fun?', *Soo?* 'Is (that) so?' (vs statement *Soo da*: we have noted the omission of *da* in questions); however, *ka* appears, for example, when followed by *ne* or *na*, as we shall see below.

Yo is an assertive particle, used to add emphasis to statements, proposals and requests: *Ikanai yo* '(I)'m not going', *Ii yo* '(That)'s fine', *Ikoo yo* 'Let's go', *Soo da yo* '(That)'s right', *Soko ni oite yo* 'Put it there'. *Yo* is also used in formal speech. In informal speech, women traditionally prefer the illocutionary marker *wa*, used with statements, although this may itself be followed by *yo*: *Ikanai wa*, *Ii wa yo*, *Soo da wa*, etc. However, there are signs that the use of *wa* as a feminine assertive particle may be losing ground among younger speakers.

Ne (lengthened variant: *nee*) is a confirmatory particle that solicits agreement from the listener: 'Isn't that right?', 'Don't you agree?', 'Do you see what I mean?', 'Right?', etc. It is attached to all types of sentences: *Ikoo ne* 'Let's go, right?', *Ikanai ne* '(You)'re not going, right?', *Omosiroi ne* '(It)'s fun, isn't it?', *Soo da ne* '(That)'s right, isn't it?', *Soko ni oite ne* 'Put (it) there, OK?', etc. It may also follow the illocutionary markers discussed above, adding a confirmatory nuance: *Ikoo ka ne* 'Shall I go, I wonder?', *Ii ka ne* 'Is (it) OK, I wonder?', *Soo ka ne* 'Is (that) so, I wonder?' (note that *da* is dropped before *ka*), *Soo da yo ne* '(That)'s right, isn't it?', *Ii wa yo ne* '(It)'s OK, isn't it?', etc. Unlike the other markers, *ne* may also occur more widely, punctuating the phrases of connected speech discussed in chapter 2. This is sometimes seen in an extreme form in telephone conversations, where the speaker breaks the utterance into short phrases and seeks confirmation after each: *Zya, asita ne, Yamanakaeki no ne, higasiguti no kaisatuguti de ne,* ... 'OK, so tomorrow, right, at Yamanaka Station, right, by the gate at the east exit, right, ...'.

Finally, *na* (lengthened variant: *naa*) occurs in informal speech, chiefly with questions and exclamatory assertions. It has a soliloquizing flavour and is used more commonly by men: e.g. *Ii na* 'Gee, (that)'s good', *Samui naa* 'Gee, it's cold', *Ii ka na* 'Is (it) OK, I ask myself', *Soo ka na* 'Is (that) really so, I wonder', etc.

Coordinators

Coordinators are particles that serve to join grammatical items of the same kind, such as nouns, clauses, etc. In the resulting combination, each item has equal status.

The main notion here is 'and'. In English, *and* is used widely to coordinate items of various kinds, but Japanese uses different methods for different types of elements. *To* is used to co-ordinate nouns (unmodified and modified: *kore to kore* 'this one and this one', *kono heya to ano heya* 'this room and that room') and, unlike in English, *to* must appear between all items (*nihoNgo to eego to huraNsugo* 'Japanese, English and French'). *To* may also follow the last item in the series (*kore to kore to* 'this and this'); while this is less common, it illustrates the important principle that, like all particles in Japanese, *to* belongs with the item which precedes it, whereas English *and*, etc. fall together rather with what follows. Pauses in Japanese normally come after *to* (*kono heya to—ano heya*). 'Or' between nouns is *ka* in Japanese: *kyoo ka asita* 'today or tomorrow', *kono heya ka ano heya* 'this room or that room', etc. Another common coordinator in the spoken language is *toka*, which may be characterized as a 'representative' coordinator; it conjoins items that are presented as representative examples: *nihoNgo toka tyuugokugo (toka)* 'such things/languages as Japanese and Chinese', etc.

Clauses are *not* coordinated by *to*. The most general way to link clauses with 'and' is by means of the conjunctive (*-te/-de*) form of inflected words, but clause coordinators are also found. The most common of these is *ga/keredomo/kedo*, the basic meaning of which is 'but': these differ in style, with *ga* being the most formal and *kedo* the most common in informal speech. (*Kedomo* and *keredo* are also heard.) Compare *NihoNgo wa muzukasii kedo omosiroi* 'Japanese is difficult, but interesting', *Kinoo wa samukatta kedo kyoo wa atatakai* 'Yesterday was cold but today is warm', *SumisusaN wa igirisuziN da kedo okusaN wa huraNsuziN da* 'Smith is British but his wife is French', etc. *Si* 'and' also serves to coordinate clauses, most typically where one is presenting a list of supporting reasons ('for one thing ... , for another ... '): *Kyoo wa yameyoo. Samui si, tooi si, kazegimi da si ...* 'Let's call (it) off today. It's cold, it's a long way and (I) feel as though I've caught a cold'. Note that there is no implication of sequencing with *si*.

Subordinators

Under 'subordinators' we bring together particles which mark subordinate clauses of various kinds. These vary considerably not only in their meaning but also in the grammatical types of clauses to which they are added. Some common examples are illustrated below, with an indication of major grammatical restrictions. Further attention will be given to both clause coordinators and subordinators in our discussion of composite sentences.

kara 'because': *Ame ga hutte iru kara yameyoo* 'Let's call (it) off, because it's raining'

to (quotative): *SuzukisaN wa kuru to itta* 'Suzuki said (he) would come'

to (follows non-past forms: 'if', habitual condition): *Koko o osu to beru ga naru* 'If (you) press here, the bell rings'

made (follows non-past verb forms: 'until'): *SuzukisaN ga kuru made matu* '(I) will wait until Suzuki comes' *mo* (follows conjunctive forms: 'even if'): *Ame ga hutte mo yamenai* '(I) won't call it off even if it rains'

kara (follows conjunctive verb forms: 'after'): *Tabete kara ikoo* 'Let's go after (we)'ve eaten (not before)'

ni (follows stem forms of verbs: 'in order to', purpose with motion verbs): *MiNna eega o mi ni itta* 'Everyone's gone to see a film'

This concludes our presentation of the main types of Japanese particles. One of their notable features is that what is formally the same item may often fulfil various different functions: *to*, for example, occurs as a reciprocal and a comitative case marker, as a coordinator of nouns and as a subordinator in quotative and conditional clauses. While semantic links are sometimes apparent in such cases, it is also essential to distinguish clearly between the different grammatical uses involved.

Structural nouns

The final type of grammatical words discussed here are structural nouns. These are nouns that—although they may sometimes have other, 'regular' uses—typically occur with modifiers, rather than independently, and play important roles in the construction of sentences.

Two of the most important nouns of this type are *koto* and *no* (not to be confused with the case particle *no*). The basic meaning of *koto* is '(abstract) thing', and in its grammatical uses it is often roughly equivalent to 'fact' or 'act (of doing something)'. To illustrate with a simple example, *oyogu* is a verb meaning 'swim', and *oyogu koto* (with *oyogu* modifying the noun *koto*) corresponds to the English noun 'swimming'. One way to express capability in Japanese is to use the resulting noun phrase with the verb *dekiru* 'be possible': (*oyogu koto ga dekiru* 'swimming is possible, i.e. can swim'). *No* is similar: like *oyogu koto*, *oyogu no* translates as 'swimming' and occurs in examples such as *oyogu no ga suki da* '(someone) likes swimming'. Both *koto* and *no* thus function to turn verbs, etc. into noun phrases, which can then be used in sentences like ordinary nouns; they are often termed 'nominalizers', and we shall see further examples of their use in our discussion of complement clauses.

A quite different use of *no* is as a pronoun (i.e. a noun 'standing for' another noun) meaning 'one(s)'. In this use, *no* refers to an object, etc. that is mentioned elsewhere in the utterance, or that is otherwise identifiable from the context: *akai no* 'red ones', *aoi no* 'blue/green ones', etc. Where this *no* would follow the genitive case particle *no*, the two items coalesce, so that 'my one, mine' is simply *boku no* rather than **boku no no*: *Kono kasa wa boku no zyanai* 'This umbrella isn't mine'.

Finally, *hoo* is a structural noun that may be glossed as 'alternative (of two)'. *Hoo* occurs in situations where two choices are at issue, and it often combines with the *kotira/kotti* series of demonstratives and interrogatives, which already encode this notion: 'Which one (of two) do you prefer?' may be expressed both as *Dotti ga ii?* and as *Dotti no hoo ga ii?* Elsewhere, it makes a two-way choice explicit: *akai hoo* 'the red one (of two)', *ookii hoo* 'the big(ger) one', *suzukisaN no hoo* 'Suzuki (as opposed to another person)', etc. It also occurs in constructions with *ii* 'good, OK', roughly equivalent to English 'had better (do/not do something)': *itta hoo* is 'the alternative of having gone', *ikanai hoo* 'the alternative of not going', hence *Itta hoo ga ii* '(You) had better go'/*Ikanai hoo ga ii* '(You) had better not go'.

Simple sentences

Having reviewed inflection and some of the major grammatical words in Japanese, we move on to consider the main principles of sentence structure. We begin with simple sentences, i.e. sentences consisting of a single clause. Our approach will be to look first at skeletal structures and to indicate how individual elements of these structures can be expanded; we will then see how derived sentences may be produced through processes of affixation and finally consider some common sentence extensions.

Verbal, i adjectival and copular sentences

Every basic Japanese sentence contains a predicate, consisting of a verb, an *i* adjective or a combination of the copula and some other word (typically a noun or an uninflected (*na/no*) adjective, sometimes an adverb). Accordingly, we may divide sentences into three types: verbal, *i* adjectival and copular. Compare the following examples:

Verbal

Asuko ni mo hito ga iru 'There is a person over there, too'/ *Kuraku natta* 'It's got dark'/*Sizuka ni natta* 'It's gone quiet'/ *Okane ga nai* '(I) haven't got any money'/*Okiyoo* 'Let's get up'/*Kyoo wa satoosaN ga kuru* 'Today Sato is coming'/*SatoosaN wa kyoo kuru* 'Sato is coming today'/*Boku ga iku* 'I'll go'/ *SatoosaN wa kuruma o katta* 'Sato bought a car'/*SatoosaN wa tookyoo ni iru* 'Sato is in Tokyo'.

I adjectival

Atui 'It's hot'/*Oisikatta* '(It) was good(-tasting)'/*Sore mo yoku nai* 'That's not good, either'/*Kyoo wa samuku nai* 'It's not cold today'.

Copular

Sora ga kiree da 'The sky is beautiful'/*SuzukisaN datta* 'It was Suzuki'/*Kore wa moNdai da* 'This is a problem'/*Kore ga moNdai da* 'This is the problem'/*SumisusaN wa amerikaziN zyanai* 'Smith isn't an American'/*SatoosaN wa tookyoo da* 'Sato is in Tokyo'/*Soo da* '(That) is so'.

As we have seen, the predicate comes at the end of the sentence in Japanese; copular sentences end with a form of *da* directly preceded by the predicate noun, uninflected adjective or adverb, with no intervening particles. Other elements of the sentence precede. Basic elements typically include nouns, commonly followed by case markers indicating their semantic relation to the predicate; noun + case markers may in turn be followed by range markers (*wa/mo*, etc.), with consequent dropping of *ga*, *o* and sometimes *ni*. *Wa*, as we have noted, commonly occurs in questions about a given topic, or in statements which may be seen as answering such questions: above, *Kyoo wa satoosaN ga kuru* may be seen as answering *Kyoo wa dare ga kuru?* 'Who's coming today?', *Kyoo wa nani o suru?* 'What are (you) going to do today?', etc., *SatoosaN wa kyoo kuru* as answering *SatoosaN wa itu kuru?* 'When is Sato coming?' Similarly, *Kore wa moNdai da* answers the question *Kore wa doo?* 'How is this?' whereas *Kore ga moNdai da* answers *Nani ga moNdai?* 'What is the problem?' In such cases, the phrase marked by *wa* generally stands first in the sentence. Other basic elements may also include adjectives (as in *Kuraku natta* 'It's got dark' and *Sizuka ni natta* 'It's gone quiet').

Basic verbal sentences include hortative sentences (*Okiyoo* 'Let's get up')—as well as imperative sentences, not considered here—and may also involve a wider range of case particles than other types, especially *o*. Note the wide range of meaning of the copula with nouns: while it commonly indicates identity, it may also denote a looser associative relationship, including that of location (as in *SatoosaN wa tookyoo da*).

Expansions

Each type of element in basic sentences may be expanded. Firstly, elements may be modified: as we have seen, nouns are normally modified by adjectives or by other nouns, while adjectives and verbs (and adverbs) are modified by adverbs. The basic rule here in Japanese is that modifiers precede the words that they modify. Modifiers of nouns give further information on the nature of the entity referred to by the noun. In *SatoosaN wa kuruma o katta* 'Sato bought a car', *kuruma* can thus be expanded by nouns (marked by the genitive case particle *no*) as in *doitu no kuruma* 'a German car', *tomodati no kuruma* 'a friend's car' or by adjectives (linked by *na* or *no* in the case of uninflected adjectives) as in *atarasii kuruma* 'a new car', *kiree na kuruma* 'a beautiful car', *pikapika no kuruma* 'a sparkling (clean) car', etc. Nouns may also be preceded by articles like *kono* 'this', etc., which basically specify referents in terms of location (*kono kuruma* 'this car'), and these may co-occur with modifiers (*ano atarasii kuruma* 'that new car (over there)', etc.). Other words are generally modified by adverbs, commonly expressing the manner or degree of an action, quality, etc.: cf. *Sugoku sizuka ni natta* 'It's gone very quiet', *Okane ga zeNzeN nai* '(I) haven't got any money at all', *Hayaku okiyoo* 'Let's get up early', *Kekkoo oisikatta* '(It) was pretty good(-tasting)', *Sore mo aNmari yoku nai* 'That's not very good, either', *Sora ga monosugoku kiree da* 'The sky is tremendously beautiful'. While adverbs often occur directly preceding heads, as illustrated here, they sometimes occur earlier in the sentence. As well as *Okane ga zeNzeN nai* and *Sora ga monosugoku kiree da*, one may say *ZeNzeN okane ga nai* and *Monosugoku sora ga kiree da*, and this is the normal position for many adverbs: *Moo okane ga nai* '(I) haven't got any (more) money now' is more natural than *Okane ga moo nai.

Quantifiers, including numbers, may be introduced into basic sentences in various positions, of which two are particularly common. Firstly, perhaps as expected, they may function as modifiers of nouns, which they precede and to which they are linked by *no*: *oozee no hito* 'many people', *saNdai no kuruma* 'three cars', etc. Secondly, they may also stand directly before a verb as in *Kuruma o saNdai katta* 'I bought three cars', *Tomodati ga saNnin kita* 'Three friends came'. This occurs mainly where the noun to which the quantifier applies (here, *kuruma*, *tomodati*) is marked by the case particles *ga* or *o* (or by *wa*, *mo*, etc. with consequent dropping of these two particles): thus 'I met three friends', where the case particle required is *ni* (or *to*), is expressed as *SaNniN no tomodati ni atta* with the quantifier modifying the noun, rather than as **Tomodati ni saNniN atta*. It is important to notice that in these cases, where the quantifier may be thought of as an adverbial modifier of the verb ('bought to the extent of three', 'came to the extent of three'), the quantifier is not itself followed by case particles; this also applies in examples such as *SeNeN kureta* '(They, etc.) gave me/us 1000 yen', where there is normally no noun present. Quantifiers are often expanded by the addition, following the quantifier, of grammatical words such as *dake* 'just, exactly', *gurai/hodo/bakari* 'about' (*Kuruma o saNdai dake katta* '(I) bought just three cars', *saNniN gurai no tomodati* 'about three friends'). These words, which have several other uses, belong to a special grammatical class and are often referred to as 'restrictives'.

In verbal sentences, the predicate (i.e. the verb) may often be expanded, as we have seen, by combination with auxiliary verbs. In this case the conjunctive form of the verb is followed by the auxiliary. Thus many of the basic sentences given above can be expanded in this way: *Kuraku natte iru* 'It is dark', *Sizuka ni natte kita* 'It's gone quiet', *Okite ageyoo* 'Let's get up (for somebody's benefit)', *Kyoo wa satoosaN ga kite iru* 'Today Sato (has come and) is here', *SatoosaN wa kyoo kite kureru* 'Sato will come (for our benefit) today', *Boku ga itte kuru* '*I*'ll go (and come back)', *SatoosaN wa kuruma o katte itta* 'Sato bought a car (before he went)', etc. In most cases the addition of an auxiliary does not affect the valency of the basic verb, but *aru* and *morau* are exceptions. *Aru*, as we have seen, combines with transitive volitional verbs, as in *katte aru* '(something) has been bought (by someone)'. Such verbs typically have a valency of two, with the actor marked by *ga* and the affected entity by *o*. By contrast, the combination *katte aru*, etc. has a valency of one: the single associated noun refers to the affected entity, and this may be marked either by *ga* or *o* (cf. *Biiru ga/o katte aru* 'Beer has been bought (by someone)'). *Morau* '(I/we, etc.) receive the favour of (someone doing something for me/us)' increases the valency of the basic verb by one, since it introduces an extra participant, namely the person who performs the favour: this participant is always marked by *ni*: cf. *SuzukisaN ga kuruma o katta* 'Suzuki bought a car' and *SuzukisaN ga otoosaN ni kuruma o katte moratta* 'Suzuki received the buying of a car from his father, i.e. Suzuki's father bought him a car, Suzuki had his father buy him a car'.

Derivations

Japanese has an important set of derivational processes that apply very generally to verbs and, sometimes, adjectives. They typically result in valency changes and, thus, differences in sentence structure, and in view of their generality they are conveniently described in grammar in terms of operations which are applied to basic sentences and produce 'derived' sentences. The basic examples below all involve affixation; it is noticeable that what Japanese does here by this means, English generally achieves by the use of separate words, such as *make, can, want, look, seem,* etc.

Causative

Causative sentences in Japanese express the notion that someone makes, or lets, someone do something. They imply a certain authority on the part of the causer over the other person (the 'causee'), and they are thus commonly used with reference to the actions of parents towards children, teachers towards students, bosses towards junior colleagues, etc. Where the causer is junior to the causee (as in 'I got my father to buy me a car'), the auxiliary *morau* ('receive the favour of') is normally used.

To produce a causative sentence we must first form a causative verb. This is done by means of the suffix *-(s)aseru*, which is added to virtually all basic verbs as follows:

Class 1   *-u → -aseru* (e.g. *iku* 'go' → *ikaseru* 'make/let go', *yomu* 'read' → *yomaseru* 'make/let read'; N.B. *kau* 'buy' → *kawaseru* 'make/let buy', etc.)

Class 2   *-ru → -saseru* (e.g. *taberu* 'eat' → *tabesaseru* 'make/let eat', *iru* 'be located (of animates)' → *isaseru* 'make/let be located')

Irregulars *suru* 'do' → *saseru* 'make/let do'
　　　　　 kuru 'come' → *kosaseru* 'make/let come'

Causative verbs themselves are class 2 verbs. Since they involve the additional participation of a causer, they have a valency of one more than the basic verb. In general, the causer is marked by *ga* and the causee by *ni*: thus, basic *Kodomo ga yasai o tabeta* 'The child ate the vegetables'/causative *OkaasaN ga kodomo ni yasai o tabesaseta* 'The mother made/let the child eat vegetables'. Where, however, the basic verb is intransitive (i.e. has no centrally associated noun marked by *o*), the causee is also commonly marked by *o*: cf. basic *Kodomo ga soto de asoNda* 'The child played outside'/causative *OkaasaN ga kodomo o/ni soto de asobaseta* 'The mother made/let the child play outside'. In these cases, *o* is associated with more direct causation ('make'), *ni* with more indirect causation ('have', 'let').

Adversative

Adversative sentences are particularly common in spoken Japanese. Their basic meaning is 'someone (commonly the speaker) is adversely affected by someone else's doing something', and they thus contrast semantically with main verb + auxiliary *kureru* sentences, where someone else's action is expressed as an incoming favour.

Adversative sentences make use of derived verbs formed by the suffixation of *-(r)areru*. These are generally referred to as 'passive' verbs, since they also appear in passive sentences, comparable to English *John was hit (by James)* vs basic *James hit John*. Whereas 'passive' normally refers to sentences which are derived from transitive sentences (one cannot say *John was died, from intransitive *die*), adversative sentences have no such restriction; 'I was adversely affected by someone's dying' is a perfectly logical notion. Furthermore, unlike passives, adversative sentences introduce an extra participant into the situation, in the form of the person adversely affected (the 'victim'). Adversative and passive sentences are thus different sentence types, involving a different range of verbs. As indicated, the verbs are formed with the suffix *-(r)areru*, which features the sound *r* where the causative suffix has *s*:

Class 1   *-u* → *-areru* (e.g. *iku* 'go' → *ikareru* 'be adversely affected by somone's going', etc., *yomu* 'read' → *yomareru*; N.B. *kau* 'buy' → *kawareru*)

Class 2   *-ru* → *-rareru* (e.g. *taberu* 'eat' → *taberareru*, *iru* 'be located (of animates)' → *irareru*)

Irregulars *suru* 'do' → *sareru*
          kuru 'come' → *korareru*

Adversative verbs themselves are class 2 verbs. In adversative sentences the victim is basically marked by *ga*, the agent responsible for the adverse happening (the 'perpetrator') is marked by *ni* and other case marking is unaffected. Compare basic *Kodomo ga naita* 'The child cried'/adversative *OkaasaN ga kodomo ni nakareta* 'The mother was inconvenienced by the child's crying', *Kodomotati ga keeki o zeNbu tabeta* 'The children ate all the cakes'/*OkaasaN ga komodotati ni keeki o zeNbu taberareta* 'The mother was inconvenienced by the children eating all the cakes', *Ame ga hutta* 'It rained'/*OkaasaN ga ame ni hurareta* 'The mother was inconvenienced by it raining', etc. Note that while the perpetrator is normally a person or an animal, natural forces such as rain may also serve in this role. The nearest general English equivalent to this construction is perhaps provided by the use of *on* as in *The mother was cried on by the child*, *The mother got rained on*, etc. It is also worth stressing that the perpetrator must be distinct from the victim: if I drop a plate and it smashes, this is an inconveniencing situation for me, but there is no question of using an adversative sentence for one's own actions. Instead, the auxiliary *simau* would be used: *Watte simatta* '(I)'ve (gone and) broken (it)' or *Warete simatta* '(It) has (gone and) broken'. As noted earlier, one use of *simau* is to describe an unwanted happening, and, not surprisingly, this auxiliary commonly co-occurs with adversative verbs (*Ame ni hurarete simatta*, etc.).

True passive sentences (i.e. sentences derived from transitive sentences, without the introduction of additional participants) are more widely used in written Japanese. Where they do occur in the spoken language, they commonly involve an adverse implication since, once again, Japanese has available contrasting means (the auxiliary *morau*, etc.) of expressing beneficial actions. In passive sentences, the actor is marked by *ni*, and the affected entity by *ga*: cf. *SuzukisaN ga boku ni soo itta* 'Suzuki told me that'/*Boku ga suzukisaN ni soo iwareta* 'I was told that by Suzuki', *OkaasaN ga kodomo ni yasai o tabesaseta* 'The mother made the child eat vegetables'/*Kodomo ga okaasaN ni yasai o tabesaserareta* 'The child was made to eat vegetables by the mother'. Note that the latter example is derived from a causative verb.

In summary, Japanese has two sentence types, which we have called 'adversative' and 'passive' (other terms include 'indirect passive' and 'direct passive'). These involve different valencies and a different range of verbs. They share the same pattern of derivation (in *-(r)areru*), and in spoken Japanese the passive, like the adversative, is commonly interpreted as inconveniencing.

Potential

The most common way in which to express personal capability in Japanese ('somebody can do something') is by the use of a potential verb. These are formed from basic verbs as follows:

Class 1   *-u* → *-eru* (e.g. *kaku* 'write' → *kakeru* 'can write', *yomu* 'read' → *yomeru* 'can read', *kau* 'buy' → *kaeru* 'can buy')

Class 2   *-ru* → *-rareru*/*-reru*   (e.g. *taberu* 'eat' → *taberareru* /*tabereru* 'can eat', *okiru* 'get up' → *okirareru* /*okireru* 'can get up')

Irregulars   *suru* 'do' → *dekiru* 'can do'
             kuru 'come' → *korareru* /*koreru* 'can come'
             (*iku* 'go' → *ikeru* /*ikareru* 'can go')

Note that class 2 verbs have alternative potential forms: the longer forms (*taberareru*, etc.) are identical with the adversative/passive (but have a different valency, as we will see); the shorter forms (*tabereru*, etc.) are common in speech, but are not yet universally recognized as 'correct'. Clearly there is a change in progress in the language here, towards a single potential pattern (final *-u* → *-eru*) for all verbs. Potential verbs themselves are class 2 verbs; moreover, they are stative verbs and do not combine with the auxiliary *iru*.

Potential verbs normally behave as intransitives, i.e. they do not govern a noun marked by *o*: any nouns marked by *o* in basic sentences are marked by *ga* in potential sentences (*kaNzi o kaku* '(somebody) writes kanji'/*kaNzi ga kakeru* '(somebody) can write kanji', *niku o taberu* '(somebody) eats meat'/*niku ga taberareru—tabereru* '(somebody) can eat meat', etc.) and nouns referring to the 'possessor' of the capability are marked by *ni* or *ga* (*Kodomo ni wa niku ga taberarenai (kara)* '(Since) children can't eat meat', *Ano hito ga kaNzi ga yomenai (kara)* '(Since) he/she can't read kanji', etc.).

Desiderative

Desiderative sentences ('I want to do (something)') involve the use of desiderative adjectives, derived by the suffixation of *-tai* to the stem form of volitional verbs (*ikitai* '(I) want to go', *tabetai* '(I) want to eat', *sitai* '(I) want to do', etc.). Other forms of *-tai* words follow the normal pattern for *i* adjectives: *ikitakatta* '(I) wanted to go', *ikitakute* '(I) want to go and . . .', *ikitaku nai* '(I) don't want to go', etc. As indicated by the glosses, *-tai* words are subjective adjectives: in simple declarative sentences, they refer to the desires of the first-person ('I') and sentences such as **SatoosaN wa ikitai* 'Sato wants to go' are ungrammatical in Japanese.

Desiderative sentences show competing case-marking patterns. In the first pattern, marking is the same as in basic sentences, and *-tai* words—unlike basic adjectives—behave transitively, governing nouns marked by *o*: thus, *Watasi ga niku o taberu (kara)* '(Since) I will eat meat'/*Watasi ga niku o tabetai (kara)* '(Since) I want to eat meat'. In the second pattern, *-tai* words are intransitive, and *o* in the basic sentence is replaced by *ga* (*Watasi ga niku ga tabetai (kara)* '(Since) I want to eat meat').

Evidential

The final derivational process considered here involves the suffixation of *-soo* to verbs and adjectives, to produce sentences meaning '(someone/something) looks as if they are/do/will do (something)'. *-soo* is added to the stems of verbs and *i* adjectives and to the basic form of uninflected adjectives:

Verbs: *huru* 'fall (of rain, etc.)'/*hurisoo* 'looking as if it will fall' *i* adjectives: *oisii* 'good(-tasting)'/*oisisoo* 'looking as if it is good(-tasting)' (N.B. *ii* 'good'/*yosasoo* 'looking as if it is good')

na adjectives, etc.: *geNki na* 'in good spirits'/*geNkisoo* 'looking to be in good spirits'

-soo words themselves are *na* adjectives, and they retain basic case marking: cf. *Ame ga hurisoo da* 'It looks like rain', *Suzu-kisaN wa kaze o hiite isoo da* 'Suzuki looks to have caught a cold', *SatoosaN wa uresisoo datta* 'Sato looked happy', *Oziisan wa geNkisoo datta yo* 'Granddad looked in good spirits', etc. *-soo* may also be added to negative forms: *nai* (as the negative form of *aru* as well as in the negative form of adjectives) and *zyanai* (the negative form of the copula) produce the irregular forms *nasasoo* and *zyanasasoo*. Compare *Kyoo wa ame ga hura-nasoo da* (from *huranai*) 'It doesn't look as if it will rain today', but *Kono keeki wa oisiku nasasoo da* (from *oisiku nai*) 'This cake doesn't look good(-tasting)' and *OziisaN wa aNmari geNki zyanasasoo datta* (from *geNki zyanai*) 'Granddad didn't look in all that good spirits', etc.

Extensions

In this section we have considered different types of basic sentences, expansions of their major elements and some common derivational processes which apply to them. Here, finally, we look at a variety of common elements that may be regarded as extensions which are attached to the end of basic sentences, to produce meanings connected with the status—as truth, conjecture, probability, appearance, etc.—of the information given. These elements are added to all types of basic sentence—verbal, *i* adjectival and copular—and the chief formal complication concerns their addition to copular sentences ending in the non-past form *da*. As previously mentioned, this is an unstable form; while it is retained in some cases, we will see that before certain extensions it is dropped, or replaced by *na*.

The first extension, *daroo*, adds the meaning 'I guess, probably' to basic sentences. *Daroo* is actually a form of the copula (often termed the 'tentative' or 'presumptive') and an original *da* is omitted: cf. *SuzukisaN wa konai daroo* 'Suzuki probably won't come', *Tyuugokugo wa muzukasii daroo* 'Chinese must be difficult, I would think', *Ano hito wa nihoNziN zyanai daroo* 'He/she isn't Japanese, I wouldn't think', *Sore wa soo daroo* (with *da* dropped: cf. *Sore wa soo da*) 'That's probably so', etc. Questions with *daroo* ('Isn't that right?', 'It must be X, I suppose?') are common: *Nattoo wa dame daroo?* 'I suppose nattoo (fermented soya beans) are no good, right?' *Itta daroo?* '(I) told (you so), didn't I', *Soo daroo?* 'Isn't (that) right?' Sentence-final *daroo* is mainly used in informal male speech; female speakers, and males in more formal circumstances, generally use its more formal equivalent, *desyoo*.

Kamosirenai adds the notion of 'maybe' to the basic sentence. It is weaker than *daroo* and merely comments on the possibility of a state of affairs, rather than committing the speaker to a belief in its probability. Compare *SuzukisaN wa konai kamosirenai* 'Maybe Suzuki won't come', *Ano hito wa nihoNziN zyanai kamosirenai* 'Maybe he/she isn't Japanese', *Soo kamosirenai* (with *da* omitted) 'Maybe (that)'s so'.

Rasii is one of many forms in Japanese that have to do with the nature of the evidence for the information presented in the basic sentence. We have already seen one such form, the evidential (*-soo*), where the evidence is primarily visual. With *-rasii* (which is an *i* adjectival form), the evidence is based on second-hand sources, including reports, although it is not explicitly restricted to hearsay. Close English equivalents include 'apparently', 'one gathers that ...', 'it seems that ...', etc. Thus, whereas the statement *Kyoo wa ame ga hurisoo da* 'It looks as if it's going to rain today' is based on visual assessment of the weather, *Kyoo wa ame ga huru rasii* is likely to be based on what one has heard, or read (in a weather report, from other people, etc.). Compare *SuzukisaN wa konai rasii* 'It seems Suzuki isn't coming', *Ano hito wa nihoNziN zyanai rasii* 'Apparently, he/she isn't Japanese', *Soo rasii* (*da* omitted) 'Apparently (that)'s so', etc.

Mitai da is a *na* adjectival form; it has a wide range, but often suggests first-hand judgement on the basis of direct involvement: cf. *Nai mitai da* 'It looks as if there aren't any (e.g. after checking)', *Kaze o hiita mitai da* '(I) seem to have caught a cold', *Soo mitai da ne* (original *da* omitted) '(That) seems to be so, doesn't it'.

One of the most common, and most important, sentence extensions involves the grammatical noun *no* plus the copula *da*; in spoken Japanese this combination appears as *N da*. This adds overtones suggested by such English expressions as 'the situation is . . .', 'the thing is . . .', 'the fact is . . .', 'the reason is . . .', etc., but it is used much more widely than these. A common use is in giving explanations (*Kyoo wa okyakusaN ga kuru N da* 'Visitors are coming today (that's why we have to make preparations, etc.)', *Kaze o hiita N da* '(I)'ve got a cold (that's why I'm taking this medicine, etc.)'), and it is also widely used in preparatory statements which set the scene for questions, further exposition, reservations, etc.: *Kyoo wa okyakusaN ga kuru N da kedo syokuzi wa naNzi ni suru?* 'Visitors are coming today—what time shall we have the meal?', *Kinoo hazimete nattoo o tabeta N da kedo aNmari suki zyanakatta* 'I ate nattoo yesterday for the first time—but I didn't like it much'. However, it is also used simply in emphasizing factuality ('I'm telling you'), and its effects are often reflected by differences of stress and intonation in English. The form *da* is replaced by *na* before this extension, i.e. the expected sequence *da N da surfaces as *na N da*, as in *Soo na N da* '(That)'s right (i.e. that's the explanation for the situation, etc.)'. This extension is also used in questions; as we have seen, sentence-final *da* is generally omitted in questions, and in such cases *N* reverts to its full form *no*. Once again, this is particularly common in questions seeking explanations (as in 'why'-questions), in questions seeking confirmation of factuality, etc.: *NaNde naite iru no?* 'Why are (you) crying?', *SuzukisaN wa hontoo ni kuru no?* 'Is Suzuki really coming?', *Soo na no?* 'Is (that) really so?', etc.

Finally, the extension *soo da* indicates that the sentence to which it is added is reported as hearsay ('They say that . . .',

'I hear that ...', etc.). This is not to be confused with the evidential -*soo*, which is a suffix added to the stems of verbs and adjectives. Hearsay *soo da* is added to all types of basic sentences, and a preceding *da* is retained: *Kyoo wa ame ga huru soo da* 'They say it's going to rain today', *SuzukisaN wa konai soo da* 'I hear Suzuki isn't coming', *OziisaN wa genki da soo da* 'They say Granddad is in good spirits', *Soo da soo da* 'They say (that)'s true'. *Soo da* is often replaced by the more conversational *tte*: *SuzukisaN wa konai tte* 'They say Suzuki isn't coming', *Ano hito wa nihoNziN zyanai tte* 'They say he/she isn't Japanese', *Soo da tte ne* 'That's what they say, isn't it'.

Compound and complex sentences

In addition to simple sentences, every language has composite sentences, which may be regarded as being formed by combining simple sentences together in various ways. Thus in English *Jack fell down* is a simple sentence, which may appear in composite sentences such as *Jack fell down and broke his crown; Jack, who fell down, broke his crown; When Jack fell down he broke his crown; Jill saw Jack fall down*, etc., involving grammatical adjustments of various kinds. The different simple-sentence-like parts of composite sentences are called 'clauses', and are divided into 'main' and 'subordinate' clauses according to their function in the combined sentence.

Subordinate clauses play a dependent role, for example as modifiers or as elements filling valency slots of verbs: in the examples above, *who fell down, when Jack fell down, Jack fall down* are all subordinate clauses. Typically, subordinate clauses may not stand alone as simple sentences in their own right, as a result of the grammatical modification which they undergo in the course of their incorporation into the composite sentence; however, this is not always the case: in *Jill said Jack fell down, Jack fell down* is a subordinate clause even though it may constitute a simple sentence as it stands.

Clauses that are not subordinate are main clauses. Main clauses may typically stand alone as independent sentences but, once again, there are exceptions: in *Jack fell down and broke his crown, broke his crown* is a main clause, but it is incomplete as a simple sentence. As far as sentences containing two clauses are concerned, as above, a combination of main clause + main clause produces a compound sentence, while main clause + subordinate clause produces a complex sentence: *Jack fell down and broke his crown* is thus a compound sentence, and the rest are complex.

In combining simple sentences we shall see that Japanese uses the full range of grammatical devices including inflection, grammatical words (coordinators, subordinators and structural nouns) and word order. Once again, we will find considerable differences from English. Indeed there are cases where Japanese, unlike English, does not combine sentences at all. A notable example is alternative questions, which pose two options and ask for a choice between them: *Shall we eat now, or (shall we eat) later?, Is Smith American, or (is he) Canadian?* etc. Here English links the two clauses in a compound sentence with *or*, but Japanese asks two (simple) questions: *Ima taberu? Ato de taberu?, SumisusaN wa amerikaziN? KanadaziN?*

Compound sentences

Japanese forms compound sentences mainly with the coordinators *ga/keredomo/kedo* 'but' and *si* ('and', 'for one thing'), or by means of inflection through the use of the conjunctive ('and') form.

We have already discussed the coordinators and stressed that they belong with the preceding clause, rather than with the following clause as in English. Here we may add that the range of *ga/keredomo/kedo* is much wider than that of *but*, which implies a contrast. Indeed they sometimes occur where English would use separate sentences. This is particularly noticeable where they mark a prefatory statement setting the scene for a related comment or question: *Kyoo kyabetu o katta N da kedo takaku natta ne* 'Today (I) bought some cabbage—(it)'s become expensive, hasn't it?', *Moo sugu natuyasumi da kedo doko ni iku?* 'It'll soon be the summer vacation—where shall (we) go?'

The most general equivalent of English *and* between clauses in Japanese is the use of the conjunctive form in the first clause, as in the following verbal, *i* adjectival and copular sentences:

Boku wa nihoN ni itte otooto wa tyuugoku ni itta 'I went to Japan, and my brother went to China'.
SuzukisaN wa se ga takakute kaminoke ga nagai 'Ms Suzuki is tall and has long hair'.
SumisusaN wa amerikaziN de syumittosaN wa doituziN da 'Smith is American and Schmidt is German'.

The conjunctive form is simply a linking form, and its interpretation with respect to tense, etc. depends on the later predicate to which it is linked: thus *itte* in the first sentence above is interpreted as referring to the past since it is linked to *itta* and so on. The conjunctive has an extremely wide range of use—as has *and* in English—and it also occurs in subordinate clauses as defined here. The clearest cases of compound sentences are those where, as in the above examples, the order of clauses may be reversed without affecting the overall meaning.

Complex sentences

Basic complex sentences combine a main and a subordinate clause. Subordinate clauses fall into three major types, according to their role in the composite sentence. Relative clauses (like *who fell down* in *Jack, who fell down, broke his crown*) modify noun phrases, and their function is thus similar to adjectives in this role. Adverbial clauses (*when Jack fell down*) function like adverbs and commonly express such notions as time, condition, purpose, etc. Finally, some subordinate clauses behave like nouns and occupy the valency slots of verbs: these are known as 'complement' clauses (since they serve to 'complete' the sense of the verb). In *Jill saw Jack fall down*, *Jack fall down* is a complement clause, functioning grammatically like the (pro)noun *this* in *Jill saw this*.

Relative clauses

Relative clauses, like adjectives in their modifying use, serve to give additional information about the noun(-phrase) that they modify. In English, they follow the noun and are generally introduced by words such as *who, which, that,* etc. (cf. *the man who came to dinner, the car which I bought, the woman whose bike he borrowed, the place where she grew up, the day that war broke out, the reason why I went*).

In Japanese relative clauses, like adjectives, precede the words which they modify. Moreover they are signalled purely by their position and do not make use of special grammatical words. To make a relative clause in Japanese one simply places the information directly before the noun, retaining normal word order (predicate-final) within the clause. In Japanese one says:

> *yuusyoku ni kita hito* '(the) came-to-dinner man'
> *boku ga katta kuruma* '(the) I-bought car'
> *ano hito ga ziteNsya o karita oNnanohito* '(the)
>   he-borrowed-bike woman'
> *ano hito ga sodatta tokoro* '(the) she-grew-up place'
> *seNsoo ga hazimatta hi* '(the) war-began day'
> *boku ga itta riyuu* '(the) I-went reason'

The above relative clauses all contain verbs, but they may also contain *i* adjectives (*me ga ookii hito* 'person whose eyes are big'), *na* adjectives (*eego ga zyoozu na hito* 'person who is good at English') and *no* adjectives (*itumo kutu ga pikapika no hito* 'person whose shoes are always sparkling'); they may also contain nouns followed by the copula, in which case the expected form *da* is replaced by *no*: 'the teacher who is Japanese' is thus *nihoNziN no seNsee* (rather than **nihoNziN da seNsee*) and 'the teacher whose wife is Japanese' is *okusaN ga nihoNziN no seNsee* (rather than **okusaN ga nihoNziN da seNsee*).

Japanese sometimes makes use of relative clauses where English uses adverbial clauses. This applies particularly with notions of time. Thus the equivalent of English *before* is *mae*, which is a noun ('time before') in Japanese: *before he came to Japan* is thus *ano hito ga nihoN ni kuru mae* (*mae* is always preceded by the non-past tense). Similarly, 'time, occasion' is

toki, and this is often used where English uses clauses introduced by *when*: *when one crosses the road/when crossing the road*
is *miti o wataru toki*. Note that if *when* can be interpreted as
'after', *toki* is preceded by the past tense: 'Let's buy it when we
go to Tokyo' is *Tookyoo ni itta toki ni kaoo* if we mean that we
will buy it in Tokyo, *Tookyoo ni iku toki ni kaoo* if we mean
that we will buy it e.g. to take with us on the journey.

Adverbial clauses

Adverbial clauses serve to modify predicates or larger elements
of main clauses and may be grouped into various common
semantic types such as time (cf. English clauses introduced by
when), condition (*if*), reason (*because*), purpose (*in order to*),
manner (*as*), etc. We can look at only some of these types here.
Whereas adverbial clauses in English may precede or follow
the main clause (*If he comes I'll see him/I'll see him if he comes*),
in Japanese they always precede. Japanese adverbial clauses are
signalled by inflection and by the use of subordinators.

As we have seen, the Japanese conjunctive form is basically
a linking form, broadly comparable in use to *and* between
clauses in English. Its precise interpretation depends on context: in some cases this is simply conjoining ('X is the case, and
Y is the case', etc.), and we have treated these under compound
sentences; in other cases—although the dividing line is not
always easily drawn—it is more clearly subordinating. Often
the interpretation is sequential ('X happened and then Y happened', etc.): *Kyoo wa kono sigoto o owarasete goruhu ni iku*
'Today (I) will finish this work and (then) go golfing', *GohaN
o tabete kaeroo* 'Let's eat and (then) go home', etc. The link
between a conjunctive and a main clause may also be interpreted as causal ('X happened and so Y happened', 'X is the
case and so Y is the case', etc.): *Okane ga nakute komatte iru* '(I)
have no money and (so) am in a fix', *Kyoo wa atatakakute kimoti
ga ii* 'Today is warm and (so) it feels good', *Ame ni hurarete
bisyobisyo ni natta* '(I) was rained on and (so) became soaking
wet'. Common combinations here include adjective conjunctive + *ii* ('is X and (so) it is good, i.e. is nice and X': *Kono heya*

wa hirokute ii ne 'This room is nice and spacious, isn't it') and conjunctive + *yokatta* ('X and so it was good, i.e. it was good that X': *Ame ga huranakute yokatta* 'It was good that it didn't rain', *Kyoo wa ii teNki de yokatta* 'It was good that the weather was fine today'). Finally, the conjunctive clause may be interpreted as indicating means or manner ('do X and (thereby/in this way) do Y'): *Aruite iku* '(I) will walk and (thereby) go, i.e. I'll walk (there)', *Kono ki o tukatte hoNdana o tukuroo* 'Let's use this wood and (thereby) make some bookshelves', *Damatte kaetta* '(He) said nothing and (in that way) went home, i.e. He left (for home) without saying anything'. As mentioned earlier, a 'without' interpretation is common with the negative *-naide* conjunctive form found with volitional verbs (*GohaN o tabenaide dekaketa* '(They) didn't eat and set off, i.e. (They) set off without eating'); a substitutive interpretation ('instead of') is also found here (*Kuruma ni noranaide ziteNsya de ikoo* 'Let's not get in the car, and go by bicycle, i.e. Let's cycle instead of going by car').

Other means often exist to make these notions explicit, where necessary. To emphasize sequence ('after, not before'), the conjunctive may be followed by *kara*: *GohaN o tabete kara kaeroo* 'Let's go home after we eat/Let's eat first and then go home'. Cause or reason is specifically signalled by *kara* following non-past and past, not conjunctive, forms: *Kyoo wa samui kara uti ni iyoo* 'It's cold today, so let's stay home', *Ano toki inakatta kara siranakatta* '(I) wasn't there at that time, so (I) didn't know'. Causal *kara* is sometimes used to link clauses in Japanese where English prefers two simple sentences and leaves the relationship unexpressed: *Kurai kara ki o tukete* 'It's dark— be careful'. *N de* (or *no de*, especially in writing) also signals cause. This is actually the conjunctive form of the extension *N da* (*de* being the conjunctive form of the copula), and the basic meaning of *N de* is thus 'the situation is . . . and (so)': *Ano toki inakatta N de siranakatta* 'The fact is (I) wasn't there at that time, and (so) (I) didn't know'.

Japanese has several types of adverbial clauses that overlap with conditional ('if') clauses in English. Interestingly, some of these may also be translatable by English *when*. The difference between *Let's go when Smith comes* and *Let's go if Smith comes* is that with *when* Smith's coming is assumed to be definite, whereas with *if* it is regarded as uncertain. Japanese often leaves this particular difference unexpressed, but draws other distinctions according to the relationship between the two clauses. Both the above sentences would commonly be translated by means of the so-called 'conditional' form (ending in *-(kat)tara/-dara*) in Japanese: *SumisusaN ga kitara ikoo*. Sentences with this form normally refer to specific (rather than generic or habitual) situations, where the happening/state in the subordinate clause is presented as completed/existing before the event of the main clause takes place. Their general force is thus 'On a given occasion, when/if X happened/ happens, then Y followed/will follow/would follow'. Compare *Sakki giNkoo ni ittara yasumi datta* 'When (I) went to the bank just now, it was (closed for the) holiday', *SoNna koto o sitara okorareru yo* 'If (you) do a thing like that, then people will get angry', *Ame ga huttara yameyoo* 'If it rains, then let's call (it) off', *OraNdaziN dattara eego ga dekiru daroo* 'If (they) are/were Dutch, then (they) will/would probably be able to speak English'. Note the first use, referring to a past occurrence, where the consequence is commonly unexpected ('When X happened, guess what followed').

Generic or habitual conditions are expressed by the subordinator *to*. These sentences have the force 'if/when/whenever X happens/is the case, Y follows as a matter of course': *Osake o nomu to kao ga akaku naru* 'When (I) drink alcohol, (my) face becomes red', *Kono botaN o osu to tyokoreeto ga dete kuru* 'When (you) press this button, chocolate comes out', *Yuugata ni naru to hiete kuru* 'It gets cold in the evenings', etc. Such sentences naturally have non-past forms in each clause.

A further inflected form, the provisional (ending in *(-ker)-eba*), generally indicates a necessary condition, i.e. 'provided that', 'so long as' or (in the negative) 'unless': *Kusuri o nomeba naoru* 'Provided that (you) take the medicine, (it) will get better', *Kusuri o nomanakereba naoranai* 'Unless (you) take the

medicine, (it) won't get better', *Tenki ga yokereba iku* '(I'll) go
so long as the weather is fine', etc. The provisional contrasts
with the conditional in that it focuses on the prerequisite for
a given eventuality ('What X is necessary to produce Y?'),
whereas with the conditional the interest is primarily on the
consequence ('Given X, what Y ensues?').

The provisional occurs in several characteristic uses that
reflect this focus: followed by the adjective *ii* 'good, OK' in
the main clause, it indicates a strongly recommended course
of action: *Takusii de ikeba ii* 'Provided (you) go by taxi, it's
OK, i.e. (You) should go by taxi', *Isya ni mite moraeba ii* '(You)
should have it seen to by a doctor', *KaNzi o tukawanakereba ii*
'What (you) should do is not use kanji', etc. With the past
form, *yokatta*, reference is to a counterfactual past situation
('should have done X', etc.): *Ano toki ieba yokatta* '(I, you, etc.)
should have said (so) at the time', *Tabenakereba yokatta* '(I)
shouldn't have eaten (it), I wish (I) hadn't eaten (it)', etc.
Finally, a negative provisional followed by *naranai* 'it won't
do', *dame da* 'it's no good', etc. indicates obligation: 'unless one
does X it won't do, i.e. one must do X'. Compare *NihoNgo
de kakanakereba naranai* '(I) have to write (it) in Japanese',
Motto beNkyoo sinakereba dame da yo '(You) must study more',
etc.

The conjunctive form followed by the range particle *wa*
(i.e. *te/-de wa*) also translates as 'if' and is likewise commonly
followed by *dame da* 'it's no good' or *ikenai* 'it won't do'.
Where the conjunctive form is positive, the meaning is prohib-
itive ('if one does X, it's no good, i.e. one must not do X');
where negative, the meaning is once again of obligation: *Soko
de asoNde wa dame da* '(You) mustn't play there', *Sitizi madeni
kaeranakute wa ikenai* '(I) have to be home by seven o'clock'.
Followed by the range particle *mo* (i.e. *-te/-de mo*) the conjunctive is generally translated by 'even if': *Ame ga hutte mo iku*
'(We) will go even if it rains', *Takakute mo kau* '(I) will buy
(it) even if (it) is expensive', *NihoNgo de mo yomeru* '(I) can
read (it) even if it is Japanese', *NihoNgo zya nakute mo yomeru*
'(I) can read (it) even if it's not Japanese'. These clauses are

often followed by *ii* 'good, OK', yielding sentences meaning 'It's OK even if X'/'One may X' or 'It's OK even if it's not X'/'One doesn't have to X', etc.: *Tabako o sutte mo ii* 'One may smoke', *Eego de kaite mo ii* 'One may write in English', *ZeNbu tabenakute mo ii* 'One doesn't have to eat (it) all', *Kyoo zya nakute mo ii* 'It doesn't have to be today', etc.

Finally, quotative clauses in Japanese—i.e. clauses that report what people say, think, etc.—are best described as a type of manner clause. These clauses are marked by the subordinator *to*, which we may refer to here as the 'quotative particle'. In English, clauses of this type commonly involve changes of tense: to report a past utterance, *It is raining*, English grammar requires us to replace *is* by *was* after the past tense verb in the main clause: *He said (that) it was raining*. Japanese is more straightforward here: essentially, the rule is simply to report the original words, followed by *to*. Since the original words here are *Ame ga hutte iru*, the full sentence is thus *(Ano hito wa) ame ga hutte iru to itte ita*. Note that the form *da* is retained in quotative clauses: *SyumittosaN wa huraNsuziN da* 'Schmidt is French' is reported as *(Ano hito wa) syumittosaN wa huraNsuziN da to itte ita* '(He) said that Schmidt was French'. While *yuu* 'say' is the most common verb found with quotative clauses, other communication verbs such as *kiku* 'hear' (*Ame ga hutte iru to kiita* '(I) heard (i.e. from someone) that it was raining') and *kiku* 'ask' (*Ame ga hutte iru ka to kiita* '(I) asked whether it was raining') are also found. Note that the interrogative marker *ka* appears in this last example, since the reported utterance is a question. Quotative clauses are also used to report thoughts, typically with the verb *omou* 'think': *Kyoo wa ame ga huru to omou* 'I think it will rain today'; in the negative, English typically negates the main verb (*I don't think . . .*), but in Japanese it is normal to negate the thought: *Kyoo wa ame ga huranai to omou* 'I think it won't rain today, i.e. I don't think it will rain today'. *Omou* also occurs with hortative forms in the quotative clause, the combination generally being equivalent to English 'be thinking of doing': *RaineN nihoN ni ikoo to omotte iru* 'I'm thinking of going to Japan next year', etc.

Complement clauses

Complement clauses are comparable to nouns in that they occupy the valency slots of verbs and other predicates. The main types involve the use of the grammatical nouns *koto* and *no* and—in the case of indirect questions—simple incorporation into the sentence without any special marking.

We have already introduced the structural nouns *koto* and *no*, noting that they have very general meanings ('fact', 'act', etc.) and that their main role is to produce noun phrases (i.e. to act as 'nominalizers'). *Koto*, in particular, occurs in a wide range of fixed constructions. These include the 'experiential' construction with the verb *aru* 'be located (of inanimates), exist': the Japanese equivalent of *Have you ever been to Kyoto?* is *Kyooto ni itta koto ga aru?*, literally, 'Does (your) having been to Kyoto exist?', to which the response is either *Aru* '(It) exists' or *Nai* '(It) doesn't exist', as appropriate. Non-past verbs may also occur before *koto* here, in which case the meaning relates to current habit: *Kyooto ni iku koto ga aru?* 'Do (you) ever go to Kyoto?' *Koto* also occurs with the verbs *suru* 'do' and *naru* 'become', in constructions referring to decisions or arrangements. 'Decide on X' is commonly expressed in Japanese as *X ni suru*: in a restaurant, one might say *(Watasi wa) suteeki ni suru* '(I) will have (lit. "decide on") steak'. Where one decides not on a particular object but on a course of action, this is rendered by a complement clause with *koto*: *RaineN nihoN ni iku koto ni sita* 'I have decided on going to Japan next year'. With *naru*, the meaning is that a decision or arrangement has been reached, without this being attributed to any particular decision-maker: *RaineN nihoN ni iku koto ni natta* 'It has been decided/arranged that (I) will go to Japan next year'. Both *koto* and *no* occur more generally referring to propositions, facts, actions, events, etc.: *no* tends to occur with reference to more directly perceivable or cognizable situations, *koto* (and, often, *to yuu koto* 'the fact, namely that ...', 'the reported fact that ...') in more abstract or indirect cases. Thus *no* is used with verbs of sensory perception, such as *miru* 'see': 'I saw Suzuki' is *SuzukisaN o mita* and 'I saw Suzuki leave' is

SuzukisaN ga deru no o mita. In 'I didn't know that Suzuki couldn't speak Japanese', *koto* is preferred: *SuzukisaN wa nihoNgo ga dekinai (to yuu) koto wa siranakatta*. There are also cases where both may be used: 'I realized I didn't have any money' is *Okane o motte inai no/koto ni ki ga tuita*.

As a final type of complement clause let us mention indirect questions with verbs of cognition (such as *siru* 'get to know', *wakaru* 'become clear', *wasureru* 'forget', etc.), in sentences comparable to English *I know where he is, I have forgotten when she came, I don't know whether he can speak Japanese*, etc. In Japanese, the rule once again is to go back to the basic wording of the question; the interrogative marker *ka* must be added, and the result placed directly before the verb, commonly with no other marking, although range markers sometimes appear. In the first example, the basic question is *Ano hito wa doko ni iru?* 'Where is he?'; adding *ka* to this, we obtain the sentence *(Watasi wa) ano hito wa doko ni iru ka sitte iru*. The second sentence is similar: *Ano hito wa itu kita ka wasureta*. In the last example, the basic question is *Ano hito wa nihoNgo ga dekiru?* This differs from the other examples in that it contains no interrogative term (such as *doko* or *itu*), and Japanese always converts such cases into alternative questions by the addition of *doo ka* 'or not?' (lit. 'or how?'). The full sentence is thus *Ano hito wa nihoNgo ga dekiru ka doo ka siranai*. Since *doo* is itself an interrogative term ('how?'), we may summarize by saying that all Japanese indirect questions must contain an interrogative: if it is not there originally, one supplies it through the addition of *doo*. As always, *da* will be dropped here before *ka*: *Ano hito wa nihoNziN ka doo ka wakaranai* '(I) don't know whether he/she is Japanese or not'.

CHAPTER 6

DISCOURSE

In this chapter we shift our perspective from the Japanese language system to the Japanese language in use, especially in conversation. Chapter 5 provided an account of the workings of Japanese grammar, which determine how we may combine vocabulary items in sentences in order to communicate. This account needs expanding and refining in various ways, in order to bridge the gap between the general design features of the language and the practical details of the Japanese we find in everyday use.

First we need to discuss additional manifestations of style in Japanese grammar and, in particular, to give details of the so-called 'formal' style, which involves its own set of inflectional endings. Considerations of style must also include reference to the contractions, inversions and ellipses that are a common feature of the spoken language, and which were omitted from our somewhat idealized account in chapter 5. The mechanics of conversation bring into use a special range of vocabulary items that play a central role in both the physical and social management of spoken language interaction: items used to indicate hesitation or to fill pauses, to respond to a summons, to a question, or to signal one's attention to what the speaker is saying. 'Procedural' items of this kind lie at the periphery of the regular vocabulary, but their basic importance is obvious as soon as we listen to actual conversations. The same applies to the stock of social formulaic exchanges that play an essential role in linguistic interaction in all communities. Japanese has a particularly rich array of such formulas, and their mastery is indispensable to smooth communication. This leads us to note, finally, the more general presence of a wide range of conventional routines and patterns that form part of the basic coinage of everyday speech.

Two major themes will emerge clearly from this chapter. The first is the high degree of linguistic variation found in Japanese according to social aspects of the situation of use. Both in grammar and in vocabulary, Japanese sentences directly reflect contextual features of this kind, and it is no exaggeration to say that every Japanese utterance carries social information, particularly regarding the relationship of the speaker and the addressee. This is a major factor in the difficulty of Japanese as a foreign language and in the time required for learners to approach native-like competence. The second theme is more general and concerns the importance of learning, as items, pre-programmed linguistic 'chunks' of various kinds, be they social formulas, routines for getting particular things done through language or various other kinds of set expressions which simply happen to be 'the way things are said' in Japanese. In all languages, certain options from among the manifold theoretical possibilities provided by the grammar and vocabulary are conventionalized as the 'normal' way to say certain things. Control of such expressions is an essential requirement both for natural fluency and for the comprehension of everyday speech.

Style and grammar

Style is a matter of the association between linguistic items and circumstances of use. Our presentation of Japanese grammar has focused on a somewhat idealized version of the informal spoken style, and we must now consider further common refinements to this style as well as major grammatical repercussions of other styles. As with vocabulary, a convenient framework for discussion is provided by the dimensions of medium (spoken vs written language), gender (male vs female users) and formality (informal vs formal situations, characterized in terms of the social distance between participants), although, as we shall see, these interact in various ways.

Medium

While written Japanese is far from being a single, homogeneous style, two of the most general grammatical features of the written language are a preference for longer forms of the copula (*de aru vs da*, etc.) and the use of the stem of verbs and the *-ku* form of *i* adjectives as linking ('and') forms, parallel to this use of the conjunctive form in spoken Japanese. The written-style equivalent of a spoken sentence such as *Tai wa siromi no sakana de, saNma wa aomi no sakana da* 'Tai is a white-fleshed fish, and samma is a dark-fleshed fish' is thus *Tai wa siromi no sakana de ari, saNma wa aomi no sakana de aru*, with *de ari* (the stem form of *de aru*) replacing the conjunctive form *de* and *de aru* replacing *da*; similarly, *Buta wa asi ga mizikaku, hana ga ookii* 'Pigs have short legs and large snouts' (with the *-ku* form of *mizikai* 'short') replaces *Buta wa asi ga mizikakute, hana ga ookii*.

As in the vocabulary, some grammatical items also contrast as 'colloquial' vs 'bookish': the extension *mitai da* 'it looks/ seems that', for example, is an exclusively spoken-language item which is replaced in written Japanese by its more formal counterpart *yoo da*, and the clause coordinators *keredomo/kedo* give way to *ga* in written Japanese. Variant forms may also be involved: the *i* adjective *ii* 'good, OK' has various quasi-grammatical uses and, as we have seen, the alternative non-past form *yoi* occurs in the written language (cf. the common written-language expression *X to itte mo yoi* 'It is OK even if one says X, i.e. One may say X'). More generally, written Japanese does not exhibit the various contracted variants that characterise the spoken language; this is particularly apparent with the high-frequency extension *N da*, which will typically appear as *no de aru* in the written language: cf. spoken-language *Kore ga moNdai na N da* 'The fact is, *this* is the problem' vs *Kore ga moNdai na no de aru.*

A final general feature of written Japanese is the absence of illocutionary markers; the only exception is the interrogative marker *ka*, which occurs in such common written-style extensions as *X no de wa nai daroo ka* 'Is it perhaps not the case that X ...?'

Gender

Gender-related grammatical distinctions are found chiefly in the informal spoken language and were alluded to in chapter 5. Interestingly, these centre once again on aspects of the use of the copula. Essentially, female speakers tend to omit the form *da* when sentence-final, or when followed by the illocutionary markers *yo* and *ne*; this also applies to sentence extensions such as *N da*, which appears simply as *no* (the 'full' form of *N*). Compare the following typical contrasts between male and female utterances:

Male	Female
Kiree da	*Kiree* ('(It)'s pretty')
Sizuka da ne	*Sizuka ne* ('It's quiet, isn't it')
Daizyoobu da yo	*Daizyoobu yo* ('It's OK')
Nai N da yo	*Nai no yo* ('There aren't (any)')
Soo na N da yo	*Soo na no yo* ('(That)'s right'), etc.

Paradoxically, one situation in which *da* is retained in women's speech is before the feminine illocutionary marker *wa* (*Kiree da wa*, *Soo da wa ne*, etc.). Outside *da*, women also tend to avoid the sentence-final use of the tentative form of the copula, *daroo*, and of hortative forms of verbs in *-oo/-yoo* (*ikoo*, *tabeyoo*, etc.) in favour of their respective formal variants, *desyoo* and *-masyoo* forms (*ikimasyoo*, *tabemasyoo*, etc.).

Formality

Important topics here are the formal style and, secondly, various contractions and other refinements found chiefly in informal speech.

Formal style

Of central concern to grammar is the presence in Japanese of a formal style, marked by special inflections in verbs, *i* adjectives and the copula. The formal style serves to encode social distance between the speaker and the addressee. While the use of the informal style is natural within the family and between close friends, when addressing children and when addressing oneself—as in exclamatory utterances such as *Itai* '(That) hurts, Ouch!', *Komatta naa* 'Gee, (that)'s a problem'—the formal style is normal outside this range. Terminology varies widely in this area: 'plain/familiar/direct' (for our 'informal' style) and 'polite/distal' (for our 'formal' style) are common alternatives; more widely, this whole area is often referred to under the heading of 'addressee honorifics' (since the forms encode aspects of the social relationship between the speaker and the person addressed), as opposed to the 'referent honorifics' discussed earlier (which encode deference on the part of the speaker to the person talked about). While referent and addressee honorifics are in principle independent (in theory, one can show deference to a person under discussion in an informal conversation between friends), in practice referent honorifics tend to occur in formal style: as noted in chapter 4, the RP referred to is very frequently the addressee ('you'), and in such situations deference is typically combined with social distance.

Table 6.1 Major formal inflected forms

Negative

Verbs	
Non-past *hanasimasu/mimasu*	*hanasanaidesu/minaidesu, hanasimaseN/mimaseN*
Past *hanasimasita/mimasita*	*hanasanakattadesu/ minakattadesu, hanasimaseNdesita/ mimaseNdesita*
Hortative *hanasimasyoo/ mimasyoo*	
I adjectives	
Non-past *huruidesu*	*huruku naidesu, huruku arimaseN*
Past *hurukattadesu*	*huruku nakattadesu, huruku arimaseNdesita*
Copula	
Non-past *desu/de arimasu*	*zyanaidesu, zyaarimaseN/de naidesu, de arimaseN*
Past *desita/de arimasita*	*zyanakattadesu, zyaarimaseNdesita/de nakattadesu, de arimaseNdesita*
(Tentative *desyoo/de arimasyoo*)	

The main formal-style inflected forms are illustrated in table 6.1. Formal-style inflections chiefly involve finite forms: non-past and past, hortative (for verbs) and, in the case of the copula, the tentative extension (informal-style form: *daroo*). For verbs, the positive endings *-masu* (non-past)/*-masita* (past)/ *-masyoo* (hortative) are added to the stem form; this rule holds for all verbs except special subject-honorific verbs ending in *-aru* (*irassyaru*, etc.), where the stem ends in *-ari* (e.g. *irassyari*) but the *r* is dropped before these inflections (*irassyaimasu/*

nasaimasu/ossyaimasu/kudasaimasu). The copula shows the special forms *desu* (non-past)/*desita* (past)/*desyoo* (tentative). For *i*
adjectives and all negative forms (which inflect like *i* adjectives), the basic rule is to add *desu* to the informal forms.
Alternative negative forms are made for verbs by the addition
of *-maseN* (non-past)/*-maseNdesita* (past) to the stem, and for *i*
adjectives and the copula by the substitution of *arimaseN/*
arimaseNdesita for *naidesu/nakattadesu*; these alternatives are
somewhat more formal. Finally, the copula shows the expected 'long' forms that appear, for example, with intervening
range particles.

   Most importantly, use of the formal style involves the
replacement of some, but not all, inflected forms by formal-
style forms. This is clear from the fact that non-finite forms
(stem, provisional, conjunctive, conditional, representative)
do not have commonly occurring formal-style counterparts.
For example, the formal-style versions of *Gozi ni okite tegami
o kaita* '(I) got up at five o'clock and wrote a letter' and *Ame
ga huttara doo siyoo?* 'What shall we do if it rains?' are *Gozi ni
okite tegami o kakimasita* and *Ame ga huttara doo simasyoo?*, with
the finite forms alone carrying the stylistic distinction. More
generally, the basic rule is that only the final predicate in a
sentence is marked for style. In a composite sentence, non-final
predicates generally remain unchanged even if they are finite
forms; thus, *SuzukisaN wa konai daroo* 'Suzuki probably won't
come', *Kyoo wa okyakusaN ga kuru N da* 'Today visitors are
coming', *Boku ga katta kuruma wa yoku hasiru* 'The car that I
bought runs well', *Ano hito wa ame ga hutte iru to itte ita* 'He
said that it was raining', *Ano hito wa nihoNgo ga dekiru ka doo
ka wakaranai* '(I) don't know whether he can speak Japanese',
which all contain two finite forms, have formal-style counterparts *SuzukisaN wa konai desyoo, Kyoo wa okyakusaN ga kuru
N desu, Boku ga katta kuruma wa yoku hasirimasu, Ano hito wa
ame ga hutte iru to itte imasita, Ano hito wa nihoNgo ga dekiru
ka doo ka wakarimaseN*. The chief exceptions to this are compound sentences with the coordinators *ga/keredomo/kedo* 'but'
and *si* 'and, for one thing', and complex sentences with the

subordinator *kara* 'because': in these sentences, the predicate preceding these particles is often (although not always) marked for formal style. Thus *NihoNgo wa muzukasii(desu) kedo omosiroidesu* 'Japanese is difficult, but interesting', *Kyoo wa yamemasyoo. Samui(desu) si, tooi(desu) si . . .* 'Let's call (it) off today. It's cold, and it's a long way . . .', *Ano toki inakatta(desu) kara siranakattadesu* '(I) wasn't there at that time, so (I) didn't know', etc. As expected, the use of formal-style variants in non-final predicates increases the overall formality of the sentence.

Given this situation, it is desirable in the interests of clarity to distinguish between terms used for styles ('informal'/ 'formal', etc.) and terms used for inflected forms (i.e. *iku* vs *ikimasu*, *da* vs *desu*, etc.). If we use 'plain' (*iku/da*, etc.) and '*desu/-masu*' (*ikimasu/desu*, etc.) to label forms, the general rule is that informal style uses plain forms, while formal style uses *desu/-masu* forms in sentence-final predicates and plain forms elsewhere. This distinction is also important when we consider the use of these forms in written Japanese. Normal usage in the written language is to employ plain forms (including, as we have seen, longer forms of the copula), but the stylistic flavour of this usage is 'impersonal' rather than 'informal'; where *desu/-masu* forms are used in writing (as, for example, in certain kinds of popular instructional works), the effect is of a more direct appeal to the reader, i.e. of a 'personal' rather than of a 'formal' style. This may be summarized as follows:

	Spoken language	Written language
Plain forms	Informal style	Impersonal style
Plain + *desu/-masu* forms	Formal style	Personal style

Finally, we must not forget the presence of a further spoken-language style, namely extra-formal (also termed 'hyperpolite'), marked chiefly by the use of the small set of special verbs noted in chapter 4 (*gozaimasu* vis-à-vis *aru*, etc.) as well as the special copula *de gozaimasu*. As noted, this style is nowadays restricted in use, being chiefly associated with formal speeches and announcements and certain service encounters. Once again it is useful to distinguish between the style ('extra-formal') and the special linguistic items involved (e.g. '*degozaimasu*' or '*gozaimasu*'). Here, too, not all eligible predicates are replaced by these items, and there is the additional factor that certain set expressions incorporating these forms (e.g. *Arigatoogozaimasu* 'Thank you', *Omedetoogozaimasu* 'Congratulations', which also incorporate older *i* adjective forms) are by no means restricted to extra-formal style.

Even leaving aside the extra-formal style, the presence of two widely used styles with major grammatical repercussions poses important questions for the teaching of Japanese. At the introductory level, one may choose to begin with plain inflected forms (and thus informal-style sentences), with *desu/-masu* forms (and thus formal style, but restricted to simple sentences) or with both forms together (with corresponding attention to both styles). Traditional teaching materials have tended to begin with *desu/-masu* forms. This has the advantage that the forms themselves are easily learned (especially if negative forms are restricted to the *-maseN/-maseNdesita* alternatives), and typical foreign learners are more likely to be addressed in, and to need to use, formal style. Even in formal style, however, plain forms are incorporated in the alternative *-naidesu/-nakattadesu* negative forms, and they are of course required as soon as one considers auxiliary expansions or composite sentences. In chapter 5 we discussed Japanese grammar purely in terms of informal style, which involves a greater initial burden in terms of inflectional complexity but a correspondingly smooth transition into formal style. This approach more closely mirrors the acquisition of styles by native speakers. The third option, i.e. teaching both types of forms together, involves the greatest formal complexity but permits attention to the dynamics of the two major styles from the outset. These are nicely reflected in commonplace utterances such as *Haitta! Hairimasita!* (spoken by a television commenta-

tor reacting to a successful rugby conversion): here *Haitta!* is
a semi-exclamation addressed, as it were, to the commentator
himself ('It's there!'), while *Hairimasita!* is more reflective and
addressed to the viewing public ('X has kicked the conversion').

Contractions

The topic of style in grammar leads us to consider various
other common 'departures' from the somewhat idealized presentation of chapter 5. These involve the spoken language and,
typically, the informal style. They may be grouped under the
three headings of contractions, inversions and ellipsis.

Contractions refer to certain common sequences of grammatical items that frequently occur in a phonetically reduced
form. Many involve conjunctive forms, ending in *-te* or *-de*,
before auxiliaries or particles:

$$-te/-de + iru \quad \rightarrow -teru/-deru$$
$$-te/-de + oku \quad \rightarrow -toku/-doku$$
$$-te/-de + simau \rightarrow -tyau/-zyau$$
$$-te/-de + wa \quad \rightarrow -tya/-zya$$

The reduction of *-te/-de* + *iru* is almost universal in informal
speech and common even in formal style: *Nani siteru?* 'What
are (you) doing?', *Kagi mottenakatta kara* '(I) didn't have the
key, so . . .', *Mada yoNdenai* '(I) haven't read (it) yet', *SuzukisaN wa doko ni suNderu ka sittemasu ka* 'Do (you) know where
Suzuki lives?', etc. For contractions of *-te/-de* + *oku*, cf. *Kattoita
hoo ga ii* '(We)'d better buy (it)', *Koko ni oitokoo* 'Let's just put
(it) here (for now)', etc. The contractions *-tyau/-zyau* are
highly characteristic of Tokyo informal speech and they have
a wide range of use. Care is needed with their formation,
particularly in contrasting cases such as *kite simau → kityau*
('come') vs *kitte simau → kittyau* ('cut'). Compare *Kowaretyatta
yo* '(It)'s (gone and) broken down', *Kore, sutetyau?* 'Shall (we)
throw this out?', *Ame ni huraretyatta* '(I) got rained on', etc.
Finally, reduction of *-te/-de wa* to *-tya/-zya* has given rise to
the usual spoken negative forms of the copula (*zyanai* vs *de*

wa nai, etc.). More generally, we have seen that conjunctive form + *wa* translates as 'if', and these contractions are common before such forms as *dame/ikenai* 'no good, it won't do', etc.: *Ittya dame yo* 'If (you) tell (them), it's no good, i.e. (You) mustn't tell (them)', *Mainiti sinakutya naranai* 'If (one) doesn't do (it) every day it won't do, i.e. (One) has to do (it) every day'.

Among other common contractions, the negative provisional ending *-nakereba* is often reduced to *-nakya* in speech, especially in the common sequence *-nakereba naranai* 'it won't do unless . . . , i.e. one must do . . . , it must be . . . ': *Kyoo wa gozi madeni kaeranakya naranai* '(I) must be home by five o'clock today', *Eego de kakanakya naranai* '(One) must write (it) in English', etc. The quotative particle *to* often becomes *tte* (*te* after *N*) in informal speech: *Suzuki tte yuu hito* 'a man who is called *Suzuki*', *naN te yuu hoN* 'a book called what?', *Ano hito wa naN te itta* 'What did he/she say?', etc. As it stands, this is not a contraction; however, the same forms are also found in place of the sequence *to yuu*, notably in the combination *X tte koto* 'the fact that X' (from *X to yuu koto*): *SuzukisaN wa nihoNgo ga dekinai tte koto wa siranakatta* '(I) didn't know that Suzuki couldn't speak Japanese'. Finally, the regular contraction of *no da*, etc. to *N da* in spoken Japanese has been noted, and *N* is also found replacing certain other CV sequences, primarily in informal speech. For example, the particle *ni* is sometimes affected in this way, particularly before *n* (*IyaNnattyatta* '(I)'ve got fed up (with it)' (cf. *Iya ni natte simatta*), etc.), and the sequences *-teru no/-deru no/-teru N da/ -deru N da* are sometimes reduced to *-teNno/-deNno/-teNda/ -deNda* (*Nani yoNdeNno* 'What are (you) reading?', *Nikai de beNkyoositeNda* '(He)'s studying upstairs', etc.).

Inversions

'Officially', Japanese is a predicate-final language: verbs and other predicates occur as the final major element in a sentence and may normally be followed only by illocutionary markers. In conversational Japanese, however, we sometimes find that elements are 'tacked on' following predicates and illocutionary markers, and we may refer to these as inversions. Compare the following typical examples:

Nani, kore? 'What's this?' (vs *Kore nani?*)
Uti ni iru, kyoo? 'Will (you) be at home today?'
  (vs *Kyoo uti ni iru?*)
NaNzi, ima? 'What time is it now?' (vs *Ima naNzi?*)
Ano hito konai ne, tabuN 'He's probably not going to come,
  is he?' (vs *Ano hito tabuN konai ne*)

In composite sentences, the normal sequences of clauses may also be inverted:

Kyoo wa ikenai ne, warui kedo '(I)'m sorry but (I) can't go
  today' (vs *Warui kedo kyoo wa ikenai ne*)
Dame yo, ittya '(You) musn't tell (them)' (vs *Ittya dame yo*)
Eego no seNsee ga iru desyoo, se ga takai 'There's a tall
  English teacher (there), right' (vs *Se ga takai eego no seNsee
  ga iru desyoo*)

In all such cases the predicate element is spoken with the basic sentence-final intonation, and the additional items follow with a level pattern.

Ellipsis

Finally, under the heading of 'ellipsis' we refer, broadly, to the omission of understood elements from sentences. We must distinguish two levels here: firstly, ellipsis in Japanese in general (vis-à-vis other languages, such as English), and secondly, ellipsis in particular styles of Japanese (especially in informal speech, vis-à-vis other styles).

At the general level, Japanese is characterized by a high degree of ellipsis when compared with English: there is a widespread principle in Japanese that, broadly speaking, if an element can be understood from the context, it is omitted. This can be illustrated most clearly with reference to verbs. As we have seen, a given verb typically 'expects' a particular number of associated noun phrases standing in particular grammatical relationships to it, referring to central participants in the situation which it describes: thus the Japanese verb *suteru* 'throw away' expects two noun-phrases, one marked with *ga* referring to the actor and one marked with *o* referring to the discarded entity. Its English translation-equivalent similarly expects two noun phrases, one—the subject—preceding the verb in basic declarative sentences and determining verb agreement, and one—the object—following.

However, the difference between the two languages emerges clearly in examples like the following: *Koko ni atta zassi wa doko? Sutetyatta* vs *Where are the magazines that were here? I threw them away*. The Japanese response *Sutetyatta* ('Threw away') contains no noun phrases, and the identity of the actor and of the discarded entity are left to be deduced from the context. In this case the involvement of magazines is clear from the preceding question, and the fact that the speaker is the actor may be taken for granted on the assumption that no other potential actors have been previously mentioned or are otherwise implicated in the situation. In English, by contrast, there is a structural requirement that noun phrase slots be filled in such cases, in this example by pronouns referring to the speaker (*I*) and relating back to the noun phrase *the magazines that were here* (*them*). Similar examples have been seen in many of the illustrative sentences given in this book. Indeed, such is the structural pressure in English for all predicates to have an expressed subject (the main exception being in 'diary' style: *Went fishing*, etc.), that a 'dummy' subject, normally *it*, must be provided in sentences like *It's me*, *It's spring*, etc. Here *it* has no clear reference and is used simply to satisfy the linguistic pattern; Japanese has no such requirement, and the corresponding (informal) sentences are *Boku da*, etc. and *Haru da*.

In short, Japanese is free to omit noun phrases where their reference is clear. English typically uses pronouns in such cases, and the consequent lower comparative frequency of pronominal expressions in Japanese reflects a major difference in the structural cut of the two languages. At first sight this feature of Japanese seems to leave the language open to high levels of vagueness: with so much being left to be understood from context, how can we be sure who is doing what to whom? Part of the answer lies in the fact that Japanese has other linguistic means that function to reduce the possibilities in this respect.

One of these is valency patterns, in particular the tendency, noted earlier, for Japanese to distinguish formally between intransitive and transitive verbs of similar meaning: thus the English verb *break* is used both intransitively and transitively (*It broke/I broke it*), but Japanese distinguishes between *kowareru* and *kowasu*. In a language that omits noun phrases, this is an important feature, since the verb itself encapsulates more information relating to the nature of the situation involved. In response to *Razio wa doo sita no?* 'What happened to the radio?', *Kowareta* '(It) broke' and *Kowasita* '(I) broke (it)' at least make clear whether the event is presented as self-generating or as the responsibility of an actor.

Another linguistic device serving to clarify these matters is the distinction between subjective and objective expressions in Japanese, most clearly reflected in adjectives (including desideratives). As we have seen, simple sentences such as *Uresii* '(I)'m glad' and *Puuru ni ikitai* '(I) want to go to the swimming pool' refer to the experience of the speaker when used as statements; when used as questions, they refer to that of the addressee (*Uresii?* 'Are (you) glad?'). By the same token, expressions referring to the external manifestations of such experiences (e.g. *Uresisoo da* '(Someone) looks glad', *Puuru ni ikitagatte iru* '(Someone) is showing signs of wanting to go to the pool', etc.) exclude the possibility of reference to the speaker. We have noted that Japanese has other constructions indicating the source—as hearsay, etc.—of information given in sentences: these are also of general relevance here, and indeed the subjective/objective distinction is a pervasive feature of the language.

Finally, many linguistic expressions that incorporate social information serve to circumscribe reference. Honorifics are an obvious case: subject-honorifics will never refer to actions of the speaker or his or her associates, while object-honorifics commonly will do so. Verbs of giving are another: verbs like *kureru* and *ageru* incorporate information on the direction of the action (incoming/outgoing) relative to the speaker and, as we have seen, this is maintained in their use as benefactive auxiliaries: *Kaite kureta* will typically refer to an act of writing done for the speaker, *Kaite ageta* to an act done by the speaker for someone else.

As in English, predicates may also be ellipted in Japanese: cf. the responses in *Itu iku? Kyoo* 'When are you going?' 'Today' and *Tegami ga kiteru yo. Dare kara?* 'A letter has come' 'Who from?', etc. However, this does not mean that ellipsis is completely unconstrained in the language. Unlike in English, for example, the main verb may not be omitted from verb and auxiliary combinations: the negative response to *Ame ga hutteru?* 'Is it raining?' must be *Huttenai* '(No,) it's not raining' and not simply **Inai* '(No,) it's not'. Similarly, we have seen that the Japanese copula must be preceded by a lexical element: in response to *Kore wa nihoNgo?* 'Is this Japanese', one may not simply say *Da* '(Yes, it) is', but must at least say *NihoNgo da* (or *Soo da* '(It) is so'). And, importantly, predicates are not normally ellipted in formal-style speech: while *Kyoo* is an acceptable informal response to *Itu iku?*, the normal response to *Itu ikimasu ka* will be *Kyoo ikimasu*. This reflects the fact that such predicates carry important social meaning, namely the encoding of social distance through the inflection -*masu*.

As a related general characteristic, let us note here the common tendency for Japanese to leave composite sentences unfinished. This typically involves the use of a clause ending in a coordinator, subordinator or conjunctive form, with no second clause following. Thus, the typical response by Suzuki to the inquiry *SuzukisaN to yuu kata irassyaimasu ka* 'Is there a person here called Suzuki?' is *Watasi desu kedo* '(That)'s me, but . . . ', the general force of the continuation being understood as 'What can I do for you?' Compare *Kyoo wa yameyoo. Samui si . . .* 'Let's call (it) off today. It's cold and (it won't be enjoyable, etc.)', *Kyoo wa zutto uti ni imasu kara . . .* '(I)'ll be home all day today, so (you can contact me here at any time, etc.)', *Kyoo wa okyakusaN ga kuru N de* ... 'Guests are coming today, so (I have to be here, etc.)', *Tyuugokugo wa doo desu ka? Soo desu ne. HatuoN ga muzukasikute ne* ... 'How is Chinese?' 'Well, the pronunciation is difficult and (I'm having a hard time, etc.)'.

The final point concerns case markers. Here we find that spoken Japanese, and particularly the informal style, is characterized by the ellipisis of case markers in circumstances where this is not tolerated in written Japanese. These must be clearly distinguished from circumstances in which case markers are normally absent in both the spoken and written language: a clear example of this is provided by point-of-time expressions, where items like *kyoo* 'today' (as in *Kyoo iku*) normally appear without case markers, as opposed to expressions such as *zyuunizi* 'twelve o'clock', which are marked by *ni* (*Zyuunizi ni iku* '(I)'m going at twelve o'clock'). Our concern here is with cases where 'zero-marking' is normal in speech but not in writing. Even in formal style, the natural form of a question such as 'Do you have any grapefruit?' is *Gureepuhuruutu arimasu ka*: the use of *ga* after *gureepuhuruutu* is unnatural, as—in an initial question, i.e. where there is no implied contrast with other items—is the use of the range marker *wa*. The precise conditions involved in this type of ellipsis are not yet fully understood. However, it appears to be primarily restricted to the core case markers *ga*, *o* and *ni* (cf. *GohaN (o) taberu?* 'Shall (we) eat?', *Goruhu (ni) iku?* 'Shall (we) go golfing?', etc.) and to be particularly common with *o*.

Conversation and vocabulary

In addition to regular lexical and grammatical items, spoken interaction in any language draws on a range of miscellaneous expressions, both single words and idioms, that have a high frequency of use and are indispensable to the smooth physical and social management of conversation. Typically these are free-standing expressions ('interjections'), rather than structural elements of sentences, and they are most conveniently labelled in terms of their conversational function.

Fillers and responders

Beginning with more physical functions, the Japanese, like conversationalists everywhere, often pause and hesitate while speaking, and there are a variety of items which are used as fillers at such times. These include *ma, sono, ano, ee, koo*, as well as multi-word items such as *naN to yuu ka na* (literally, 'what shall (I) say?') or, more formally, *naN to iimasu ka*. These also occur in lengthened variants and in combination: *Maa sonoo naN to iimasu ka . . .* 'Well, er, erm . . .', etc. *Anoo* is often used as a hesitater introducing requests (*Anoo, sumimaseN kedo . . .* 'Excuse me, but . . .') and *ano ne* (combining appeal to the addressee) as an initiating element, for example when speaking on the telephone (*Mosimosi. Ano ne . . .* 'Hello? Look, erm . . .'). *Ee to*, sometimes followed by *ne*, often occurs at the beginning of responses: *Kono syasiN wa itu no desu ka. Ee to ne . . .* 'When were these photos taken?' 'Let me see . . .'.

Basic responders are *hai/ee/uN* 'right' and *iie/ie/iya/uuN* 'not right', arranged in descending order of formality. These items signal agreement or disagreement with the content of what is said, irrespective of whether this is positive or negative in *form* (unlike English *yes* and *no*): cf. *Kyoo uti ni iru?* 'Will (you) be at home today?' *UN, iru* 'Yes, (I) will'/*UuN, inai* 'No, (I) won't', but *Kyoo uti ni inai?* 'Will (you) not be at home today?' *UN, inai* 'No, (I) won't/*UuN, iru* 'Yes, (I) will'. As here, these responders are normally accompanied by a following predicate. In response to nominal sentences these are commonly *Soo da/Soo desu* '(It) is so' and *Tigau/Tigaimasu* '(It) is different': *Kore wa nihoNgo desu ka* 'Is this Japanese?' *Hai, soo desu* 'Yes, it is'/*Iie, tigaimasu* 'No, it isn't'. Other common responders include *Soo?/Soo desu ka* 'Is that so?, I see', and *Soo (da) ne/Soo desu ne* 'That's right, isn't it'. In response to questions, this latter response functions as a filler and indicates reflection by the speaker ('Well now, let me see . . .'): cf. *Eego to tyuugokugo to dotti ga muzukasii?* 'Which is (more) difficult, English or Chinese?' *Soo da ne, tyuugokugo no hoo ga muzukasii ka na* 'Well, let me see, maybe Chinese is (more) difficult'. *Saa* 'Well now; I wonder' has a somewhat similar function, but indicates doubt or uncertainty: *Saa, dotti ga muzukasii ka na* 'Gee, which is (more) difficult, I wonder', *Saa, wakaranai* 'Gee, (I) don't know'.

Many responders, including *hai/ee/uN, Soo?/Soo desu ka, Soo (da) ne/Soo desu ne* are also used as 'chimers' (known as aizuchi in Japanese). These are items 'thrown in' by the listener at regular intervals—often in response to pauses punctuated by *ne*—to signal continuing attention to and acknowledgement of what the speaker is saying. Their use is much more frequent than that of comparable vocal signals in English: silence in a listener in Japanese will generally be assumed to indicate lost contact and will invite confirmatory utterances of *Ne?* 'Right?', 'Are you with me?' or (on the telephone) *Mosimosi* 'Hello?' Other common chimers include *hee* and *hoo* (both indicating surprise, admiration, etc.), *hoNto?* 'really?', *naruhodo* 'is that a fact?', etc.

Hai/ee/uN also occur as checkers, used to request repetition or clarification of what has been said ('What's that?', 'What did you say?'). In this use they are pronounced with rising intonation and, in the case of *hai* and *ee*, with a final glottal stop.

Connectors

Connectors are another important type of discourse item. They serve to link sentences to preceding sentences in various semantic relationships and thus do not occur at the beginning of a discourse. They normally occur sentence-initially. Common connectors used in conversation include the following:

Sequence/addition: *sore kara* 'in addition', *sosite* 'and', *sositara* 'when that happened', *sore ni* 'on top of that, for another thing'

Cause/reason: *de* 'and (so)', *sore de* 'and (so)', *da kara/desu kara* 'and so, therefore'

Substantiation: *datte* 'the reason I say this is'

Contrast: *da kedo* 'however', *sikasi* 'but', *de mo* 'even so'

Condition: *soNnara* 'if that's the case', *sore zya* 'in that case', *zyaa* 'in that case'

Social formulas

All languages have a stock of routine expressions associated with commonly recurring social situations. These often occur (as 'greetings' and 'farewells') at the beginning and end of social encounters, or as conventional formulas expressing or accompanying such acts as thanking, apologizing, requesting, etc. These expressions are both easy and difficult for foreign learners. They are easy in the sense that, as fixed routines, they can be learned as unanalysed chunks, and they provide the learners with readily available 'moves' in the conduct of every-day social interaction. The difficulties relate to the rules for their use, both with respect to the nature of the act which they perform (requesting, offering, etc.) and to the precise details of the social situations in which they are appropriately used. As in other areas, we must expect various kinds of mismatches between Japanese and English here: not only will given formulas in the two languages rarely, if ever, coincide in use, but one language may have a formula where the other has none, preferring non-formulaic expression of the same idea, or even leaving the idea unexpressed. Differences in the repertoire and use of formulas are found even within the English-speaking world, reflecting the high cultural content of these expressions: *Cheerio*, as an informal farewell greeting, occurs chiefly in British English; *Good day* 'means' different things ('hello' vs 'goodbye') in different national varieties of English; British speakers use *Sorry* in a wider range of situations than Australian speakers; and so on.

Impressionistically, Japanese has a large number of formulas of this kind, and their use is a salient feature of social encounters. While their control is thus a major factor in successful social interaction, this generally requires English-speakers to learn additional distinctions of form and use; these expressions lie at the centre of linguistic etiquette and protocol, and it is important to get them right. Social formulas are commonly used in pairs, i.e. as elements in exchanges, so that it is also important to learn appropriate patterns of response. Formally, many Japanese formulas incorporate honorifics and/or extra-formal-style forms (*gozaimasu*, etc.), and several have more or less elaborate variants, correlating with differences in formality; in the examples below, more formal variants are listed first.

Clearly, an exhaustive survey of Japanese social formulas cannot be attempted here, and we must be content to point out some major contrastive features among some of the most common expressions. Among greetings that relate to the time of day we find *Ohayoogozaimasu/Ohayoo* 'Good morning', *KoNniti wa* 'Hi (used during the day)', *KoNbaN wa* 'Hi (used after dark)' and *Oyasuminasai/Oyasumi* 'Good night', but these differ considerably in their social circumstances of use. *KoNniti wa* and *KoNbaN wa*, for example, are out of place in formal situations; moreover, unlike *Ohayoo(gozaimasu)*, they are not normally used in regularly recurring contexts, such as between work colleagues. Only *Ohayoo(gozaimasu)* and *Oyasumi(nasai)* are used among family members, the latter expression being used when retiring for the night. In all cases, echo responses, i.e. repetition of the greeting by the receiver, are appropriate. Special leave-taking and returning exchanges are used in the home. When, for example, leaving for school, the departing member says *Itte mairimasu/Itte kimasu* 'Bye, I'm off', the response being *Itte (i)rassyai* 'Bye, off you go'; on returning, the greeting is *Tadaima* 'I'm back', and the response *Okaerinasai/Okaeri* 'Welcome home'.

OgeNki de irassyaimasu ka/OgeNki desu ka/GeNki? 'Are you well?' is only used to greet an acquaintance one has not seen for some time; in this respect, 'Are you keeping well?' is a closer English equivalent. A common formal response is *Okagesama de* 'Yes, thank you', followed by a reciprocal enquiry. Similarly, there is no general-purpose farewell greeting. *Sayoonara/sayonara* is quite limited in use, being relatively informal and employed chiefly by children and young people. *OgeNki de* 'Keep well' is used to farewell people one will not see for some time. For more mundane occasions informal *Zya mata* 'See you', *Zya mata asita* 'See you tomorrow', etc. are available, and *Oyasumi(nasai)* 'Good night' is often an appropriate farewell later at night. *Situreesimasu* can be used both at the opening and at the conclusion of a formal visit, and *Osaki ni situreesimasu/Osaki ni* 'Excuse me for leaving, etc. ahead of you' is used to remaining participants when withdrawing before the end of an encounter—including when leaving one's place of work ahead of other colleagues.

Pardon-seeking and apologetic expressions include the informal *GomeNnasai/GomeN* 'Sorry', the more formal *Situreesimasita/Situree* 'Pardon me', and the more profuse *Moosiwake gozaimaseN/Moosiwake arimaseN* 'My apologies'. *Situree desu ga/Situree desu kedo* is used to preface an intrusive enquiry: 'Forgive me for asking, but ...'. *SumimaseN* 'Excuse me for imposing on you' is chiefly used to acknowledge a social imposition; it has a past version, *SumimaseNdesita* 'Excuse me for imposing on you (on that occasion, etc.)', and both are frequently elaborated by combination with the adverb *doomo* (*Doomo sumimaseN/Doomo sumimaseNdesita*). These expressions are very widely used, and they often occur in situations where English uses expressions of thanks—for example, on receiving a gift from a visitor, etc. In such cases Japanese chooses to apologize for the trouble one has caused the other person, although it is not inappropriate to accompany this with thanks (*Doomo sumimaseN. Arigatoogozaimasu*). *SumimaseN* also frequently accompanies requests; a more formal equivalent here is *Osore irimasu*.

The basic expressions of thanks is *Arigatoogozaimasu/Arigatoo* which, like *SumimaseN*, has a past-tense counterpart (*Arigatoo-*

gozaimasita 'Thank you (for an elapsed favour)') and is commonly combined with *doomo*. As indicated above, it does not always coincide in use with English *Thank you*, sometimes being replaced or at least accompanied by expressions of apology. It is also inappropriate in certain specific situations, such as in expressing thanks for a meal, where the regular expression is *Gotisoosama desita/Gotisoosama* 'Thank you for the meal'. *Otukaresama desita/Otukaresama* 'Thank you for your efforts' is used to express thanks for work or other contributions of effort, and can also be used to farewell a departing colleague at the end of the working day. When meeting or contacting acquaintances, it is customary to refer to a previous encounter by such expressions as *SeNzitu wa doomo arigatoo gozaimasita/ SeNzitu wa doomo gotisoosama desita/SeNzitu wa doomo situree simasita* 'Thank you/Pardon me for the other day' as appropriate or, more informally, *Konaida wa doomo* 'It was good to see you the other day'. English makes less use of such expressions, but they indicate the importance in Japanese etiquette of the explicit linguistic acknowledgement of continuing social relationships and obligations. *Konaida wa doomo* also illustrates the widespread use of the word *doomo* as a less elaborate expression of thanks and/or apology.

Responses to both apologies and thanks may take the form of denials of the need for these acts, as in the formal *Doo itasimasite* 'Not at all' or in *Iie, iie* 'Don't mention it'. *Kotira koso* 'It's me who should apologize to you/thank you' may also be used and followed itself by an expression of apology or thanks.

Polite offers and invitations commonly feature the word *doozo*, whose range is narrower than that of English *please*, which is also used in requests. Thus visitors to one's home may be welcomed with *Doozo oagari kudasai* 'Please come in', set at ease with *Doozo goyukkuri* 'Please stay long/longer' and farewelled with *Mata doozo* 'Please come again'. It is also used alone, often accompanied by appropriate gestures, where English uses *Please sit down, Please help yourself, Please go ahead*, etc. *Doozo yorosiku* 'Pleased to meet you' is used in formal introductions, its literal force being to invite favourable treatment on the part of the addressee. The most common formula associated with polite requests is *Onegaiitasimasu/Onegaisimasu*. This often occurs as a closing expression where a request has been made and agreed to, and in such cases it too is commonly combined with *yorosiku*: *Yorosiku onegaisimasu* 'Thank you for your (anticipated) help'.

Finally, to end this section let us note specific formulas associated with New Year (*syoogatu*), the major annual Japanese festivity. There are two basic expressions here, one used before New Year and one after. The first is *Doozo yoi otosi o omukae kudasai/Doozo yoi otosi o* 'Best wishes for the coming year', which is exchanged as a farewell greeting between participants who do not expect to meet or talk again before New Year. Once the New Year has arrived, the greeting *Akemasite omedetoogozaimasu/Akemasite omedetoo* 'Happy New Year' is exchanged on first contact. With appropriate addressees, this is often combined with *Kotosi mo doozo yorosiku onegaiitasimasu* 'I request your continuing favourable treatment this year' with, once again, explicit reference to social ties.

Phraseology

Except where they are single words, the social formulas discussed above meet the definition of idioms; they are formally restricted (and often otherwise irregular) and, typically, their usage cannot be deduced automatically from the meanings of their components. Their number can be readily multiplied, and they are particularly clear examples of expressions which must be described, and learned, as chunks.

This 'chunking' principle is of much wider relevance to language-learning. Even where expressions are not, strictly speaking, idioms, it is so often the case that, out of the various possibilities theoretically permitted by the stock of vocabulary and the rules of grammar, one particular combination is accepted and used by native speakers as *the* conventional way to say a certain thing. Thus the normal way to ask the time in

Japanese is *Ima naNzi desu ka* (*Ima naNzi?* or *NaNzi, ima?* in informal speech), incorporating the noun *ima* 'now', rather than simply *NaNzi desu ka*. The latter sentence is equally grammatical (and may be used, for example, to ask the time of some event under discussion), but the former is the 'expected' form in this particular case. Such examples highlight the importance of 'usage', and their contribution to smooth communication is obvious. We may refer to this general area—i.e. the selection of one means of expression, out of various theoretical candidates, as normal usage—as 'phraseology'.

Mastery of phraseology in effect calls for the control of a range of language chunks, of various types and sizes. Thus *Ima naNzi desu ka* needs to be learned as a single sentence, as do similar examples such as *Kyoo wa naNniti desu ka/ Kyoo naNniti?* 'What's the date (today)?' etc., where differences of detail from English are again apparent. The force of phraseology is also reflected in the selection of particular patterns or expressions as set ways of doing certain things with language, and again different languages vary here. This may be illustrated by requests, i.e. utterances which seek to get people to do things. Requests differ from commands, which also seek to do this, by being phrased in a more 'polite' way. Once again, in theory there are many ways in which this might be achieved, but in practice languages make use of a limited range of devices which are conventionalized for this purpose. Thus English often uses interrogative sentences introduced by *Can you ...? Could you ...? Would you ...? Would you mind ...?* etc., which may be combined with words such as *please* to produce requests of various levels of politeness: *Can you deliver it? Could you turn the radio down, please? Would you take this away? Would you mind moving your car?* etc. Japanese, too, commonly uses interrogative sentences to make requests but, unlike in English, potential expressions are not used directly in this way: *Todokeraremasu ka/Todokeru koto ga dekimasu ka* 'Can (you) deliver (it)?' are unnatural sentences in Japanese and are only interpretable in their literal sense, i.e. as enquiries about the addressee's ability to perform the action. Instead, requests in Japanese typically make use of benefactive auxiliaries that explicitly refer to the performing of an action for the benefit of the speaker. Compare the following more common patterns, arranged roughly in ascending order of politeness:

Todokete kureru?	'Will you deliver it for me?'
Todokete kurenai?	'Won't you … ?'
Todokete kuremasu ka	'Will you … ?'
Todokete moraemasu ka	'Can I receive your delivering it?'
Todokete kudasaru?	'Will you kindly … ?'
Todokete kudasaimasu ka	'Will you kindly … ?'
Todokete kudasaimaseN ka	'Won't you kindly … ?
Todokete itadakemasu ka	'Can I respectfully receive your delivering it?'
Todokete itadakemaseN ka	'Can I not respectfully receive … ?'
Todokete itadakenai desyoo ka	'Could I not respectfully receive … ?'

As illustrated, different degrees of politeness are achieved by selection between plain vs *-masu* forms (e.g. *kureru/kuremasu*), neutral vs honorific auxiliaries (*kureru/kudasaru*), positive vs negative forms (*kureru/kurenai*), auxiliaries of giving vs (potential) auxiliaries of receiving (*kureru/moraeru*) and direct vs tentative questions (*itadakemaseN ka/itadakenai desyoo ka*), and, naturally, these are appropriate in different situations. Broadly speaking, requests in *-te kureru/kurenai* are used in informal situations, including those within the family. *-te kuremasu ka* and the more indirect *-te moraemasu ka* are suitable for non-familiar requests where minimal elaboration is required, such as by customers in most service encounters; assuming that the request illustrated is being made in such an encounter, these are the most appropriate of the forms given in this context. Patterns with the auxiliary *kudasaru* appear to be more common in women's speech; this applies particularly to the form

-te kudasaru?, which combines deference (conveyed by the subject-honorific) with informality (conveyed by the plain form). Finally, patterns with *-te itadakeru* are standard in formal requests where honorifics are being employed; we have seen that the benefactive use of verbs of receiving (i.e. *morau/ itadaku*) is often a problem area for English-speaking learners, and these patterns featuring the potential need careful attention. Note also that these later patterns are generally too elaborate for the situation envisaged here: although safer, 'over-politeness' is no less incongruous than 'under-politeness', and the ability to adjust politeness 'downwards' when required in Japanese is no less important than control of the more formal patterns in this area.

Similar illustrations could be provided for a range of other general 'speech acts', such as commands, invitations, suggestions, etc. Once again, we would find that certain patterns carry the imprimatur of accepted usage and, as with the request frames illustrated above (*-te kureru?*, *-te itadakemasu ka*, etc.), these need to be learned as chunks.

The workings of phraseology extend far beyond examples of this kind, taking in, for example, such matters as the preference in Japanese usage for expressions like *mae no kuruma* 'the car in front' where English equally permits personal reference (*the car/guy/fellow in front*) in the same (traffic) situation. Phraseology is clearly a major component of native competence. Its message for learners is that they need to pay serious attention to 'chunks' that carry the stamp of usage—be these sentences (*Ima naNzi desu ka*), sentence-frames (*-te kureru?*) or various kinds of phrases (*mae no kuruma*). Its message for teachers is clearly to reinforce the need for exposure to realistic, situationally sited Japanese.

References

The following is a highly selective list of reading and reference materials arranged according to the topics of this book.

Language and setting

E. O. Reischauer, *The Japanese Today*, Charles E. Tuttle, Rutland, Vermont and Tokyo, 1988, is a balanced, comprehensive survey of modern Japan and its historical background which should be read by all students of Japanese. M. Shibatani, *The Languages of Japan*, Cambridge University Press, 1990, is a wide-ranging theoretical treatment that includes a good summary of current work on the genetic status of Japanese.

Sound

T. J. Vance, *An Introduction to Japanese Phonology*, SUNY Press, Albany, New York, 1987, is an excellent survey, although it is perhaps not a beginner's book.

Writing

W. Hadamitzky and M. Spahn, *Kanji and Kana*, Charles E. Tuttle, Rutland, Vermont and Tokyo, 1981, may be recommended as a beginning kanji manual for English-speaking learners. It covers the 1945 jooyookanji and contains a lucid account of the workings of the Japanese writing system. Among full-sized kanji-English dictionaries, indispensable for more advanced learners, M. Spahn and W. Hadamitzky, *Japanese Character Dictionary*, Nichigai Associates, Tokyo, 1989, lists close to 6000 kanji and has the highly useful feature of permitting composite words to be looked up under any of their constituent kanji. In this respect it is superior to A. N. Nelson, *The Modern Reader's Japanese–English Character Dictionary*, Charles E. Tuttle, Rutland, Vermont and Tokyo, 1974 (2nd revised edition) (close to 5000 kanji), which long reigned supreme in the field and is still an excellent dictionary. Finally, J. Halpern (ed.), *New Japanese–English Character Dictionary*, Kenkyusha, Tokyo, 1990, is a recent addition which is somewhat less comprehensive than these works but contains a vast amount of lexicographical information on the kanji script. A recommended textbook specifically aimed at teaching English-speaking learners to read Japanese is E. H. Jorden and H. I. Chaplin, *Reading Japanese*, Yale University Press, New Haven and London, 1976, which systematically introduces the kana scripts and 425 kanji. It assumes some familiarity with the spoken language.

Vocabulary

A. Miura, *Japanese Words and Their Uses*, Charles E. Tuttle, Rutland, Vermont and Tokyo, 1983, is a reliable work which gives a good indication of the type of extended treatment of Japanese vocabulary items required by English-speaking learners; its only limitation is its size, which permits coverage of 300 items. Representative general monolingual Japanese dictionaries include *Reikai Shinkokugo Jiten*, Sanseido, Tokyo, 1990 (3rd edition) (aimed at Japanese secondary students: 45 000 entries), *Shin Meikai Kokugo Jiten*, Sanseido, Tokyo, 1989 (4th edition) (concise: 70 000 entries) and *Gakken Kokugo Daijiten*, Gakushukenkyusha, Tokyo, 1978 (larger: 100 000 entries).

Grammar

The most comprehensive treatment is S. E. Martin, *A Reference Grammar of Japanese*, Yale University Press, New Haven and London, 1975. This is a magnificent work which, while not for the beginner, is readable as well as instructive and contains a wealth of attested examples. Among textbooks, A. Alfonso, *Japanese Language Patterns* (2 vols), Sophia University, L.L. Center of Applied Linguistics, Tokyo, 1966, is a valuable reference, notable for its illuminating treatment of a wide range of grammatical structures. E. H. Jorden and M. Noda, *Japanese: The Spoken Language* (3 vols), Yale University Press, New Haven and London, 1987–90, together with its accompanying video materials, is an innovative and systematic course in modern spoken Japanese that gives full attention to accentuation and to discourse factors. Finally, S. Kuno, *The Structure of the Japanese Language*, MIT Press, Cambridge, Mass., 1972, is an insightful and readable account of a range of grammatical topics.

Discourse

O. Mizutani and N. Mizutani, *How to be Polite in Japanese*, Japan Times, Tokyo, 1987, may be recommended as an accessible survey of general aspects of spoken interaction in Japanese. *Nihongo Notes 1–10*, Japan Times, Tokyo, 1977–90, by the same authors, contain much valuable information on discourse matters. A. M. Niyekawa, *Minimum Essential Politeness*, Kodansha International, Tokyo, 1991, is a recent guide to (addressee and referent) honorifics which is especially helpful with respect to situational aspects of use.

Index